Amusing Grace

hilarity &
hope in the
everyday
calamity of
motherhood

Rhonda Rhea understands the pressures moms face and the brief snippets of time available for spiritual renewal. *Amusing Grace* allows for a woman's reality with a fast read, entertaining stories and poignant messages that will lift your spirit and enrich your soul.

—Marita Littauer, President, *CLASServices Inc.*
Speaker/Author: *You've Got What It Takes* and *Love Extravagantly*

HOMELIFE readers have made Rhonda Rhea's monthly department a must read! Now you can feast on her humor, wit, and wisdom as she serves up biblical truths and applies them to life with *Amusing Grace.*

—Sam House, Editor-in-Chief
HOMELIFE Magazine

Rhonda Rhea brilliantly ties the joy of the Lord together with those little "joys" of life that can cause parents to pull our hair out! Sure to put a smile on your face and have you doubled-over from laughter, this is *Amusing Grace* indeed!

—Jeff Caporale, Editor
Living Light News

If God doesn't have a sense of humor, then let me off the earth! Thank God that He does! And Rhonda Rhea proves it by making us laugh and cope with the oftentimes insanity of 'smotherhood'. I couldn't resist! Rhonda will bring tears to your eyes, but I guarantee you'll welcome the kind that makes you feel like you can appreciate 'smotherhood'.

—Kathy Collard Miller, Best-selling author/speaker
Daughters of the King; Princess to Princess

Just when you thought you had enough chaos in your life, along comes Rhonda Rhea—an amazingly funny and insightful woman who offers hope in the midst of motherhood mayhem. *Amusing Grace* reminds us that God is faithful even when Junior, a bottle of ketchup, and your newly carpeted living room collide. Don't miss this treasure trove of sanity and grace—you're going to need it!

—Ginger Kolbaba, Managing Editor
MARRIAGE PARTNERSHIP Magazine

If you're a mother, you're bound to love Rhonda's sometimes hilarious, always entertaining spin on her life as a mom of five—and her observations on God's presence in the thick of it! *Amusing Grace* will help you lighten up, laugh, and learn more about God's wisdom and grace as you tackle the joys and challenges of mothering.

—Jane Johnson Struck, Editor
TODAY'S CHRISTIAN WOMAN Magazine

Who can't relate to *Amusing Grace*! Rhonda Rhea both entertains and inspires as she weaves Scripture and prayer into the hilarity of her true-to-life tales. What a great gift of inspiration to uplift the highest calling—motherhood.

—Debra D. Peppers, Ph.D.
National Teachers Hall of Fame and Radio/Television Host

Amusing Grace will no doubt tickle your funny bone and touch your heart. Rhonda Rhea is one of those rare communicators with the ability to make you laugh out loud one moment and consider a life-changing thought the next. I highly recommend this book.

—Jeff Large, Senior Online Editor
Lifewayonline.com

Amusing Grace

hilarity & hope in the everyday calamity of motherhood

Rhonda Rhea

www.cookcommunications.com/life

Life Journey™ is an imprint of
Cook Communications Ministries, Colorado Springs, Colorado 80918
Cook Communications, Paris, Ontario
Kingsway Communications, Eastbourne, England

AMUSING GRACE
© 2003 by Rhonda Rhea

First Printing, 2003
Printed in the United States of America

1 2 3 4 5 6 7 8 9 10 Printing/Year 07 06 05 04 03

Senior Editor: Janet Lee
Editor: Marianne Hering
Cover Design: RJS Design
Interior Design: RJS Design

Unless otherwise noted, Scripture quotations are taken from the HOLY BIBLE: NEW INTERNATIONAL VERSION®, NIV®. Copyright © 1973, 1978, 1984 by International Bible Society. Used by permission of Zondervan Publishing House. All rights reserved.

Scripture quotations marked "NKJV" are taken from the New King James Version. Copyright©1979, 1980, 1982 by Thomas Nelson, Inc. Used by permission. All rights reserved.

All verses taken from the King James Version of the Holy Bible are marked (KJV).

Library of Congress Cataloging-in-Publication Data

Rhea, Rhonda.
  Amusing grace : hilarity and hope in the everyday calamity of
motherhood / by Rhonda Rhea.
     p. cm.
  ISBN 0-7814-3532-3
  1. Mothers--Religious life. 2. Christian women--Religious life. I.
Title.
BV4529.18 .R48 2003
248.8'431--dc21
                           2002004657

contents

• • • • •

Part V: Grace for Head Scratchers

Part VI: Grace to Love Without Bellyaching

Part VII: Grace through His Humongous Love

dedication

• • • • •

To Richie—my encourager, teacher, friend, counselor, mentor and honey—and a walking daily model of the amazing grace of God.

And to Andrew, Jordan, Kaley, Allie, and Daniel, who keep the life of grace wonderfully amusing and who continually provide truckloads of great material. Thanks, kids, for the great life lessons you've taught me along the way. I love you dearly.

acknowledgments:
· · · · ·

Mega-thanks to Jim Watkins—teacher, writing instructor, humor guru, King of the Web and, by his own admission, "threat to society"—who has given loads of rookie writing counsel and help without ever rolling his eyes.

Great hugs of appreciation to Jan Johnson for her "you can do this" speech and for knowing when to "get in the face" of a novice with just the right encouragement.

Giant thanks to Jim Wilson for caring enough to give guidance and appropriate nudges in the right writing directions and for always knowing when to "sound the charge."

More thanks and hugs to talented and patient editor extroidinaire, Janet Lee, for sorting through countless emails and for graciously answering bajillions of annoying questions—without even losing her witness.

Very special thank yous to my incredible team of prayer warriors. Their faithful, fervent prayers have availed a book—and so much more. Blessings to you, my dear friends:

Janet Bridgeforth
Liz Clayton
Toni Hiles
Alberta Hutslter
Cindy Layman
Sheila McMichael
Ann Trail

introduction

• • • • •

"Mom, I accidentally swallowed 83 cents!"

"Mom, can you get this truck wheel out of my nose?"

"Mom, the puddle outside sucked my tennies right off my feet!"

"Mom, I can't get my army men out of the toaster. What's that smell?"

Motherhood is a great adventure. A wonderful and incredibly *tiring* adventure. Some days, it's a wonderful and incredibly tiring adventure that comes packaged with an Exedrin headache.

Does anyone else find it's a great stress-reducer to hear that other moms are experiencing the same adventures—and the same toaster disasters? I thought so! There's comfort in knowing we're not alone. There's even greater comfort in a hefty dose of perspective from God's Word. Second Timothy 3:16–17 tells us that scripture is God-breathed and that it has multi-fruitful uses in our lives. We're told in verse 17 that it's God's Word that will help us become "thoroughly equipped for every good work" (NIV). It's God's Word that equips us even in the Exedrin moments to make our mothering into a "good work."

We moms thrive on sound encouragement in our walks with Christ. Biblical motivation to live a life that blesses our Father is like our medicine. *Amusing Grace* is written with a heart's desire to enable moms to take the life-giving medicine of God's Word with a spoonful of laughter.

My hope is that you can find a few familiar happenings with a chuckle or two tucked into each chapter, then find some helpful spiritual encouragement to make the time you invest in reading this book a fruitful and profitable investment. The scripture included guarantees a healthy dose of truth—just what the doctor ordered!

Motherhood comes with new demands every day. Those good doses of truth can keep us spiritually healthy—ready to handle the everyday calamity/adventure with grace. You might even like to let a chapter or two be a day's devotion when you need a spiritual charge on a busy day (and when do moms have any other kind of day?). This book is my Rx for all moms. So take two chapters and call me in the morning, my friends.

And may God's rich, amazing and even often *amusing* grace be yours.

part one

Grace in the Minivan

*Focusing on Christ
in the busy-ness of life*

chapter one

· · · · ·

From Start to Finish

H ave you ever had one of those days when nothing gets done? It's not that you don't start anything, and it's not that you don't work hard from sunup to sundown, but at the end of the day, everything looks, well … the same.

You find that while you were cleaning the peanut butter off the living room windows, one of your kids threw up in the toaster. You ready the last little body for church, but then you find that the first child you dressed has spent the balance of his time trying to cover the cat with pudding. Do I even need to mention the laundry? Unless you have naked people running around your house, it's clearly never finished.

Then you empty your bank account paying the bills knowing that, though the paycheck is history, the bills are destined to be fruitful and multiply. Like the Terminator, "they'll be back."

I feel your pain. And I have some encouragement for you in your unfinished business: We can rest in the knowledge that we won't have these kinds of chores in heaven. Surely bathtub rings, fruit punch carpet stains, and assorted ring-around-the-collar situations all came with the curse of sin. Evil stuff. It's not that I don't think we'll have jobs to do in Glory Land; it's just that I'm quite sure heaven must be an ammonia-free zone. We're promised "no more tears," remember? Sounds ammonia-free to me. No scrubby-bubbles. No Toilet Bowl man. Nope, no tears. I'm thinking probably not even any chemically induced watering eyes.

I'll also encourage you with the news that we can cope in the here and now even feeling like so much of what we do is left hanging. (Don't worry, hanging in this context has nothing to do with putting away laundry.) Do you know when we're the most frustrated about not finishing or accomplishing anything? It's when we're struggling in our own strength to do the finishing, and when we're focusing on the wrong accomplishments. Everything that's really important in life is already finished by the "Author and Finisher" of our faith. When we surrender and let the Finisher do the finishing and the Completer do the completing, we can kick off our shoes and stop sweating the never-ending bills, dust bunnies, and laundry.

The Book of Hebrews puts it this way: "Now may the God of peace who brought up our Lord Jesus from the dead, that great Shepherd of the sheep, through the blood of the everlasting covenant, *make you complete* in every good work to do His will, working in you what is well pleasing in His sight, through Jesus Christ, to whom be glory forever and ever. Amen" 13:20–21 (NKJV, *emphasis added*). He is the Completer of every good work in us, and even more importantly, the Completer of our very hearts. "He who has begun a good work in you will complete it," we're told in Philippians 1:6 (NKJV). And "you are complete in Him" is the message of Colossians 2:10 (NKJV). Did you notice the passage in Hebrews refers to the Father as the God of peace? Imagine! Peace in the midst of your unfinished business!

And think about this. When the Father completed His redemptive plan for us through the sacrificial death of His Son on the cross, the three words that rang across eternity were "IT IS FINISHED." Looking at forever from His point of view puts the pudding-covered cat in perspective. Time with our children is a wink in the light of eternity. Let's decide to enjoy every minute—even when we're having a bad laundry day and the kids are running around half-naked.

You can shrug away the muddy socks you found under the sofa—even if you did find a fish stick inside of one. Yes, even if you can't remember the last time you had fish sticks. Rest in knowing the Father has completed the works that make life worth living and eternity something to look toward with great joy and anticipation. Rejoice in knowing no one can add the "finishing touch" the way our Father does. And he's working in our lives from start to finish.

As for this chapter … I'm finished!

"In the meantime His disciples urged Him, saying, 'Rabbi, eat.' But He said to them, 'I have food to eat of which you do not know.' Therefore the disciples said to one another, 'Has anyone brought Him anything to eat?' Jesus said to them, 'My food is to do the will of Him who sent Me, and to finish His work.'"

John 4:31–34, NKJV

chapter two
. . . . .
Life in the Fast-Food Lane

I 'd like to squelch the rumor circulating the area that if my husband wants to hide something from me, he puts it in the oven. Totally untrue. My husband would never hide anything from me.

But something could sit in my oven undetected because I do spend weeks at a time living in the fast-food lane. Maybe like me you've found yourself stuck in a "fast-food Star Trek time-warp loop" of some kind. Have you ever gotten to the end of a week and realized you hadn't used silverware? The activity-loaded lifestyle we've adopted drives us right into this pickle. And I do mean "drives" us. When school started, I entered my car. I've hardly seen still ground since. I'm thinking my letter carrier might deliver to my minivan if it weren't moving so much faster than his truck.

Has drive-through mania hit you? You drive through for a burger on your way to drive through for a prescription, then drive through for a drop-off at the cleaners before dropping off kids at ballgames and ballet classes. You drop off papers, projects, payments—you name it. Sadly, we usually end up driving through for the Lard-Burger Special or the Cholesterol Combo. I've thought about saving time and applying the burger directly to my hips. I hate to think about it, but we all know it's probably better for us to toss the burger and eat the bag.

Even if you have a path that's well worn from one drive-through to another, let me share with you the exciting news that you can have perfect direction—even when you feel you're running in circles. Yes, even when the hubbub is making you crazy and you worry you might be a couple of fries short of a Happy Meal, you can have direction. Proverbs 3:6 says, "In all your ways acknowledge him, and he will make your paths straight." Verse 5 gives us the secret: trust. Not trust in what we can plan or figure out on our own, but wholehearted trust in the Lord and His plan for our path. "Look to the Lord and his strength; seek his face always" (1 Chronicles 16:11).

Here are some worthy goals for us: to trust Him wholeheartedly, to acknowledge Him in all we do, to seek Him for strength, and to see everything we do as an offering. I've added a couple of personal goals for myself. First, to use my minivan time as prayer time. You can too. Just don't close your eyes. Secondly, I'm planning at least one home-cooked meal (a boxed version) for my family. You may see a slight dip in the stocks of the major fast-food chains. That's okay. I have bigger fish sticks to fry.

"For the LORD gives wisdom;
From His mouth come knowledge and understanding;
He stores up sound wisdom for the upright;
He is a shield to those who walk uprightly;
He guards the paths of justice,
And preserves the way of His saints.
Then you will understand righteousness and justice,
Equity and every good path."

Proverbs 2:6–9, NKJV

chapter three

· · · · ·

Would You Like Fries with That?

ost of us agree we're too busy. But what should get cut from the
schedule? I've heard many of you quickly volunteering to give up
cooking dinner. I'm deeply moved by your willingness to sacrifice.

I have to confess I've wondered if home cooking is really all it's cracked
up to be. My pantry if full of handy-dandy, boxed, microwavable, foolproof,
make-'em-in-a-minute-and-a-half dinners. Maybe you have some too. Don't
make the same mistake I did. I read some of the labels. They read almost
exactly like the ingredients on my shampoo bottle.

Chemicals and preservatives topped the lists of ingredients in all my
favorites. I'm an optimist. I'm assuming since preservatives are designed
to make things last longer, I should live to be at least 214.

Yet I do have some reservations. I've seen plastic artificial flowers.
Artificial intelligence is probably mostly plastic too. So what is artificial
flavor? And if "all natural" means "from the earth," on what planet do they
harvest the artificial, "un-natural" ingredients?

The general rule is if it tastes good, it's not allowed. I still wonder if we
should toss the contents and make a casserole with the box. Cardboard at
least has plenty of fiber. With the right sauce we really might have something here.

Whatever we decide to do with the dinner hour, there is another hour
we just can't afford to cut. Unfortunately, it seems to get the ax first, sometimes without even a conscious choice. It's an activity that's infinitely
more important than dinner. (I've got your attention now, don't I!)

I'm talking about our spiritual food. On those busy days, our time with the Lord in prayer and Bible study is the meat that gives us the energy to correctly handle all the quick decisions and extra stresses. Do you want real satisfaction? Cut out the massage and the brow waxing if something has to go, and leave in your quiet time with the Lord.

Don't let this get around, but I tend to snack when I have my quiet time. There are little hunks of crumbs between the pages of my favorite passages. If I turned my Bible upside down and gave it a good shake over the dining table, I could probably just set out the silverware and serve dinner (Aha! I CAN make dinner without using a box). I don't think that's what's meant by feasting on the Word, though.

There is sweet satisfaction in feasting on His daily special. Psalm 63:5 testifies: "My soul will be satisfied as with the richest of foods; with singing lips my mouth will praise you." The Bread of Life always satisfies. No additives needed. Your time on your knees and in His Word is all you need for a great spiritual meal. He gives you the kind of meal that never follows up with, "Would you like fries with that?"

And unlike after eating some of those frozen Chinese dinners, you won't feel empty again in an hour!

"I understand more than the ancients,
Because I keep Your precepts.
I have restrained my feet from every evil way,
That I may keep Your word.
I have not departed from Your judgments,
For You Yourself have taught me.
How sweet are Your words to my taste,
Sweeter than honey to my mouth!"

Psalm 119:100–103, NKJV

chapter four
· · · · ·
The Wonder Years

We had five babies in seven years. I know some of you overachievers have had more. I'm deeply impressed by your fortitude.

They really were the wonder years—mostly because I sometimes wonder how we did it. We were basically in survival mode.

There were ten (count 'em, ten) straight years of diapers. There were also months when my husband couldn't stand up in his pulpit without discovering (usually midsermon) that he was sporting some sort of crust, slime, or other baby scum on his lapel. Interesting baby factoid: Neckties never recover from baby barf.

Getting ready for church was no small accomplishment. I always seemed to find a hole in the little ruffle-bottom tights and twelve shiny black shoes, but only two that matched. My husband was a big help—until he decided to add an 8 a.m. service to the Sunday morning lineup. He says it was to extend the church's ministry. That's another thing I've wondered about those years. You don't suppose he "extended his ministry" so he wouldn't have to help me get all those kids ready, do you?

I moved a lot of the readying to Saturday nights. In addition to the regular bath-time agenda, I added the clothes safari, some Saturday-night ironing and (this was a biggie) nail clipping. ONE HUNDRED LITTLE NAILS! No kidding—do the math. I still have nail flashbacks.

There were days I was too exhausted to appreciate the real wonder. Other days, I was overwhelmed by the blessing. I recently found this fill-in-the-blank poem I wrote back then. If you're a new parent, you can fill in the blanks in your sleep. You've probably found you can do many things in your sleep. Welcome to survival mode.

Ready or Not

The kids tossed the bowl of sugar.
My hair caught all the mess.
Then I noticed a big green _____
On the shoulder of my dress.

Oatmeal got my young son goopy,
But he wiped himself on me.
Baby's diaper drizzled _____
All down my whole right knee.

The children aren't trying to be naughty,
But, oh, the damage they do!
The baby's nose was _____
So there's slime on my left shoe.

At least there's still my new scarf.
It's pretty and brightly flowered.
But wait, there's baby _____
Now crusty and rather soured.

But I've made it to church with my cuties.
They've not even a hair astray.
I look quite the sight from my duties;
Still, I'd have it no other way.

So while I call some of them "flashbacks," I call all of them cherished memories—because I cherish my children. Still, it's all just a glimpse of our Father's love for us. First John 3:1 says, "How great is the love the Father has lavished on us, that we should be called children of God! And that is what we are!" We can't imagine a love bigger than the love we have for our babies. Yet God uses that very love to teach us about His love for us.

If you've given your life to Christ, you are God's precious child. Isn't that a wonder?! Living in His love is glorious—and it never stains!

"I pray that out of his glorious riches he may strengthen you with power through his Spirit in your inner being, so that Christ may dwell in your hearts through faith. And I pray that you, being rooted and established in love, may have power, together with all the saints, to grasp how wide and long and high and deep is the love of Christ, and to know this love that surpasses knowledge—that you may be filled to the measure of all the fullness of God."

Ephesians 3:16–19

chapter five

· · · · ·

To-Do or Not To-Do?

I 'm a mega-list person. In my book, lists are a vital part of life. Sometimes I get carried away and start making lists of my lists. Now that's embarrassing. There's probably a 12-step program. I'm intrigued that they'll need to list the steps.

I love what a list does for me on an overwhelming morning. It helps me sort out all the "have to-dos" from the "wish I had time to-dos." Sometimes I even try to convince myself that I don't have to actually do the "have to-dos." I figure it should be enough that I thought to write them down.

Still, one of my favorite things about lists is the satisfaction of the "check-off" (no, not the Star Trek guy). I love to make checkmarks. I even write down to-dos that I've already to-done—just for the joy of checks. My list might start off something like, "(1) Get up." I've checked that one today. What a sense of accomplishment.

You may have guessed that I'm not a list person because I'm organized. "Get organized" is on every one of my lists. I'm a list person because I'm not organized by nature and because I forget everything I don't write down. Now we're back to embarrassing.

The sad thing about a to-do list is that it can get incredibly intense in a big hurry. My to-do list for this week included things like: get groceries, cut gum out of cat's fur, pick up dry cleaning, clean potato chips and tennis shoes out of toilet, buy birthday gifts, get new shoes for kids, salvage daughter's favorite blouse from computer printer, schedule dentist appointments, buy new computer printer, plan nervous breakdown … you know, the usual. I'm kidding about that last one. I don't have nearly enough time for a nervous breakdown.

I know I mentioned the embarrassment of list dependence, but I lost a lot of that when it hit me: God is a list person too. He didn't write to-do lists because He forgets. He wrote to-do lists because we forget. Many of His lists are sweet reminders. Some are stern warnings. All are vital for life.

One of my favorites is the "love list" in 1 Corinthians 13:4–8: "Love is patient, love is kind. It does not envy, it does not boast, it is not proud. It is not rude, it is not self-seeking, it is not easily angered, it keeps no record of wrongs. Love does not delight in evil but rejoices with the truth. It always protects, always trusts, always hopes, always perseveres. Love never fails."

God's "love list" is a great filter for all my lists. If I remember to filter my every list, my every word, my every action, and my every thought through His list of love qualities, then I can show more of God's "fruit list" from Galatians 5:22–23: "But the fruit of the Spirit is love, joy, peace, patience, kindness, goodness, faithfulness, gentleness and self-control."

Did you notice that love topped both lists? When I'm making my own lists and I find something I've written twice, it usually means two things. I'll "list" them: (1) the listed item is something extremely important, and (2) even though this item is something very important, it's something I may have a tendency to forget.

Our Heavenly Father knows us well. He knows that we have a tendency to be selfish instead of loving. When have we ever had to write on our to-do lists, "snap at kids," "lose patience with husband," or "get short with store clerk"? Those things don't require a lot of effort. God's way requires remembering. That's one good reason I like to keep my nose planted in His Book of lists.

Romans 8:38–39 says, "For I am convinced that neither death nor life, neither angels nor demons, neither the present nor the future, nor any powers, neither height nor depth, nor anything else in all creation, will be able to separate us from the love of God that is in Christ Jesus our Lord."

Another "love list"—it's a 3-fer! This love list reminds me that even when I'm not faithful to the lists He has made for me, He is always faithful. It also reminds me that I can't put anything on my list of failures that His love can't cross right off the list. Not a check mark. A Cross.

I think I'll put that on my list of sweet thoughts to ponder. Maybe that'll help me persevere when I'm cutting gum out of the cat's fur.

"May your deeds be shown to your servants, your splendor to their children. May the favor of the Lord our God rest upon us; establish the work of our hands for us—yes, establish the work of our hands."

Psalm 90:16–17

part two

Grace in the Migraine Moments

*Focusing on the One
who is in control*

chapter six

· · · · · ·

The Road Worrior

V acation." Just mention the word and you can expect some multifaceted responses. Some vacationer-wanna-bes immediately envision enjoying a tropical breeze, basking on a beach. For other vacationers—especially those with children—it can cause flashbacks of a toddler throwing up on the map, cross-country potty stops, red slushy upholstery stains, and turning toward the backseat with a look that could stop bullets. Me? I would have to say I envision a little of both.

Most of the time, I get to choose. Will I have a warm, fuzzy, beach-type moment, or will I end up banging my head repeatedly against the dashboard? It has a lot to do with my own attitude, my vacation expectations, and my contentment level. I can choose to fuss and fret my trip away. That's when I become "The Road Worrier."

By the way, I'm writing this juicy little morsel while vacationing. At this moment, we're feeling semifuzzy. But, as you might imagine, with five kids and two adults packed into a minivan (along with enough luggage to clothe a third-world nation), the trip has not been without flashback-inducing moments. At the last several rest-room stops, I've pressed my face against the passenger side window and, just for fun, slowly mouthed the words, "Help me!" to anyone who would look. I think the authorities are looking for me in four states.

Since I'm a Texas-grown gal, I'm happy to say Texas is among those states. Vacations are bigger in Texas. They grow everything bigger in Texas (author excepted). Sadly, that does include the bugs. I'm scratching even now. Even though we slathered ourselves with drums of cancer-causing repellent, I was pretty sure we'd be toast against these Texas bugs. (Did I just mention "Texas toast"?) I was right about the bugs. It's like running into a herd of Bug-zillas. I think there are more varieties of bugs in Texas than there are in the rainforest. And they all bite. These facts might interest an entomologist, but I'm not an entomologist.

As a matter of fact, while I was reaching for my notepad to start writing, I came close to causing a major pileup on I-30. I opened my notepad and saw bug legs. My scream just about scared my husband right off the highway and on into Arkansas. But don't worry—a little CPR and he'll be just fine. The bug, however, is dead. He was already deceased when I opened my notebook. But, unfortunately for my husband, dead bug legs look exactly like live bug legs. I stopped screaming as soon as I realized the legs weren't attached to a bug body. (You may want to send those sympathy cards to my husband at home where he's recovering nicely, thank you.)

There are choices along every journey: warm, fuzzy thoughts or head-banging. Contentment or crabbiness. Resting or worrying. Learning to rest is learning to trust. And we have the same choices all along our everyday Christian journey. We can rest in the Lord and make an effort to invoke more warm fuzzies, or we can crab and worry about every bump in the road.

How did the Apostle Paul handle his bumps in the road? In Philippians 4:11 he told us that in every circumstance, he'd learned to be warm and fuzzy—content! "I have learned in whatever state I am, to be content" (NKJV). Every state (not just Texas). He was writing from prison, for pete's sake! It was most likely a prison brimming with real live bugs! If Paul could be fuzzy from prison, shouldn't I be able to keep my cool when the map won't fold?

There's one road to contentment: "I can do all things through Christ who strengthens me" (Philippians 4:13, NKJV). Trying to find contentment anywhere other than Christ won't work in any state. Right, even Texas. One more word of vacation advice: Make sure you put the trail mix in Ziploc bags instead of those fold-over things. If you ignore this warning and put it in the fold-overs anyway, then at least make sure you check the raisins before you start snacking. If they have legs, don't eat them. I call it the John-the-Baptist snack rule. (Personally, I'm not into that locust thing.) And for the record, the leg test is not a foolproof one. Sometimes the legs are not attached.

> "Finally, brethren, whatever things are true, whatever things are noble, whatever things are just, whatever things are pure, whatever things are lovely, whatever things are of good report, if there is any virtue and if there is anything praiseworthy—meditate on these things. The things which you learned and received and heard and saw in me, these do, and the God of peace will be with you."
>
> *Philippians 4:8–9, NKJV*

chapter seven
. . . . .
You're Not the Boss of Me

D o kids have a book of quotes? Do they sit around and study it, memorizing useful lines such as "You're not the boss of me," and "Make him stop looking at me!" Are there chapters in their instruction book on how to spill a drink at every meal, burp the alphabet, and forget to flush every time I have company?

Do they go to kiddie law school to study the fine-tuned legalities of "calling it"? You know how technical a calling can be. I think one of the law entries might read: "When the front seat of the family vehicle has been 'called,' said person, hereinafter referred to as the 'caller,' has subsequent claim to said front seat for and up to, but not exceeding, the designated trip. Said caller does not relinquish his call in the occurrence of a bathroom need and/or other reasonable needs for a trip back inside the house before designated car trip occurs. Should the caller, however, leave said called front-seat position for a felt-Frisbee-need and/or other related frivolous activities, caller may forfeit the front seat and the call may be thereafter negated. However, an official and irreversible 'call' of the front seat shall forthwith remain intact until such time as the caller does in fact ride in the front seat while vehicle is moving. Designated trip shall not exceed one day's drive and shall be at least to the end of the block. Said call is null and void, however, at rest-room stops when on vacation."

And we won't even talk about the entire chapter of the kid law book that would have to be devoted to determining ownership of the prize in the cereal box!

Last year I had to explain a deep concept to my five year old. We were having "a moment." I looked down into his eyes, all wide with wonder. "Do you understand?" I asked. He answered, "Mmmm hmmm." I continued, "Did you have any questions?" His response: "Yeah, I just burped through my nose. Could you hear it?" I think he got that response from the kid book.

Of course, parents seem to have a book too. In it, we would have to find such parental staples as "Do you think money grows on trees?" "Don't make me get out of this chair," and, of course, the timeless classic, "Because I said so."

Isn't it surprising that in all reality we learned all those things without any help from books? There's no kid law book. There is no 12-step plan for parents (as far as I know) on how to nag and harangue your kids.

There is an instruction book, however, that's really all we need. God's Word can shape us into the parents we need to be. It can build great kids. It's the ultimate instruction book. Jesus said in John 8:31, "If you abide in My word, you are My disciples indeed" (NKJV). If you want to be a great haranguer, keep hunting for the right how-to book. If you want to be a disciple of Jesus, check out—and abide in—His Word. And make Him the boss of you!

> *"But this is what I commanded them, saying, 'Obey My voice, and I will be your God, and you shall be My people. And walk in all the ways that I have commanded you, that it may be well with you.'"*
>
> Jeremiah 7:23, NKJV

chapter eight
·····
Hair-Raising Adventures

I s a bad hair day one of the more frustrating events of life, or what? The other day I was trying to fluff here and spray there to manage the latest 'do. As usual I was in a hurry (harried or "hair-ried"?). Nothing was going right. I ended up with helmet hair. I had to start all over by soaking my head in the sink.

When I finally finished the second round of the hair battle, I realized I'd feathered instead of fluffing and spraying. The fluff-and-spray look I'm trying for now is the look I accidentally got a couple of decades ago when I was trying for a shag. Fluff-and-spray wasn't cool back then, so I had to soak my head in the sink. Timing is everything.

Anyway, there I was—a new millennium woman—and I had feathers. I finally managed the Farrah Fawcett hairdo I wanted as a kid—a couple of decades too late. Again, timing. Farrah Fawcett's hair on my mother's face—this was scary.

I was in danger of a clinical hair depression. I had to think of something positive—and quick. I found it: No matter what I come up with hair-wise, at least I don't have to try for teenage boy hair. You want to talk about scary hair? I have a teenage son who requires new gel, mousse, and a pint of polyurethane every two days. I'm concerned one of these days the poor boy is going to fall down and break his hair.

The "in" hair for the guys these days is a shellacked top with the front sculpted straight up. Last week my son accidentally glued his hand to the front of his head. We were all pretty worried he would have to walk around school all year in a permanent salute. It's okay now, though. By the second quart of paint thinner he was free. And I think he's happy with the new color.

Grace in the Migraine Moments

Sadly, though, I'm afraid to hug the child. Even if I can get past the fumes, that hair could put an eye out. The last time I patted him on the head, the 'do drew blood.

At least he didn't have the struggles some of his friends have had. Several have accidentally snapped off the front of their hair trying to get that hedge-look happening. During a school play practice, a teenage guy ran into one of the set walls (stage left) and put a hole in it. I reminded myself it's just a stage he's going through.

Who am I, though, to point a mousse-covered finger at those who grapple with the latest styles? Farrah Fawcett feathers, remember? Over the past couple of decades, I've buzzed, permed, clipped, rolled, chipped, curled, deep-fried—you name it (and that's just the hair on my head). I know each bizarre 'do will live out its time, and then we'll all make fun of each other in our pictures ten years or so down the road. It's just a matter of time.

On the matter of time, my goal is to redeem my time for something valuable—in whatever hairstyle I'm sporting. I only get one chance to trade in each moment for something worthwhile. Like some of those infomercials for long and lovely, almost-real-looking hairpieces, it's a one-time offer—just one swap. Too much time spent on clothes, TV, computer games—yes, even hair—can yield a sad time of fruitlessness. Ephesians 5:15–17 says, "See then that you walk circumspectly, not as fools but as wise, redeeming the time, because the days are evil. Therefore do not be unwise, but understand what the will of the Lord is" (NKJV).

We don't have time for fruitlessness. The world needs us to be salt and light. There's a lot to do for Christ. Hair is probably not at the top of the list. The good news is He can use us even with helmet hair. Not even the color matters—but then we'll talk about my chemical dependence another time.

"See then that you walk circumspectly, not as fools but as wise, redeeming the time, because the days are evil. Therefore do not be unwise, but understand what the will of the Lord is. And do not be drunk with wine, in which is dissipation; but be filled with the Spirit, speaking to one another in psalms and hymns and spiritual songs, singing and making melody in your heart to the Lord."

Ephesians 5:15–19, NKJV

chapter nine
· · · · ·
The Outer Limits

My sister Gina mourned the day her youngest son was too big to fit into the grocery cart. It wasn't exactly a "my baby is growing up" kind of mourning. It was more like a prayer: "Lord, help us—Jake is free."

My four-year-old nephew makes shopping an adventure. On one trip, I watched Gina gather trail mix, coloring books, toys—enough equipment for an Iron Man triathlon. I even thought I saw rope in the trunk. I didn't ask questions.

One of the most interesting things about Jake is that he has lived all four of his years with no self-imposed boundaries. You know that sense that says, "Hey, this might not be a good idea"? Jake doesn't have that. He lives unencumbered by bothersome restrictions—pushing the outer limits to the max.

At the store, for instance, he lost us on the produce aisle. By the time we found him, there were six bites out of four apples and he was stuffing grapes in his mouth like nobody's business. I made a mental note: Weigh Jake before shopping. Then we can weigh him on the way out of the store and pay by the pound. I had to make another note later: This plan will not work if Jake swallows coins from under the deli counter.

You should've seen the cute, blond tornado tossing mega-boxes of chocolate cupcakes into the cart. Okay, I might've encouraged that one. But then he poked little Jakie-finger holes in the plastic wrap covering the hamburger. By the time we managed to grab him, he had already punctured nine two-pound packages. (My sister is now planning a cookout for her entire neighborhood. A couple more grocery store visits and it just might be countywide.)

Grace in the Migraine Moments

Next Jake found some balls in the toy section and starting chucking them in every direction. He clipped one shopper in the ear and grazed another on the forehead. He pulled a plastic bowl out of the cart, put it on his head and made a break for the pharmacy. He was already stuffing the extra balls into the blood pressure cuff when we caught up. By then I was thinking of asking a couple of those "rope" questions.

It's not that Jakie isn't actively learning about restrictions. He's lived most of this year of his life in time-out. The paddle at Jake's place seems to be perpetually warm. Some of us learn boundaries the hard way.

We've all had trouble with boundaries from the beginning. God said to Adam in Genesis 2:16, "You are free to eat from any tree in the garden." He gave perfect freedom. But then He also gave the boundaries when He said, in essence, "but not that tree over there."

There is sweet freedom inside the boundaries God has set up for us. But when we step outside of those boundaries, OUCH! Our Heavenly Father lovingly disciplines His children. Hebrews 12:9–11 tells us that "We have all had human fathers who disciplined us and we respected them for it. How much more should we submit to the Father of our spirits and live! Our fathers disciplined us for a little while as they thought best; but God disciplines us for our good, that we may share in his holiness. No discipline seems pleasant at the time, but painful. Later on, however, it produces a harvest of righteousness and peace for those who have been trained by it."

Most of us need a reminder now and then that it's much more pleasant to live within His limits. We find those limits in black-and-white written in His Word. When we go against the principles He has spelled out for us in the Bible, God uses discipline in our lives to bring us back around to those principles—He disciplines us "for our good." Verse 10 tells us that the "good" is the ability to share in His holiness.

We are spiritual farmers. Though our Heavenly Father's discipline may be painful, we can see it as plowing up hard ground and planting holiness seeds. That means that we can look forward to reaping. Did you notice the harvest? It's a harvest of righteousness and peace. Verse 9 also tells us that when we submit to the Father of our spirits, we can live. Really live. There's no better way to live than to grow and flourish within His limits, enjoying a life filled with righteousness and peace—cut the rope.

"I run in the path of your commands,
for you have set my heart free.
Teach me, O Lord, to follow your decrees;
then I will keep them to the end.
Give me understanding, and I will keep your law
and obey it with all my heart.
Direct me in the path of your commands,
for there I find delight.
Turn my heart toward your statutes
and not toward selfish gain.
Turn my eyes away from worthless things;
preserve my life according to your word."

Psalm 119:32–37

chapter ten

. . . . .

My Face Has Fallen and It Can't Get Up

T hankfulness doesn't always just happen naturally. I try to keep a "thanks program" going for myself. It's a list—sometimes written, sometimes mental—of all my thanks-worthy blessings. My children are a bright spot on the list. They add so much spice and joy into life. Of course, it's those same spicy little children that can give me some of my greatest thanksgiving challenges.

The other day, for instance, my seven-year-old studied me for a bit, then came out with, "Mom, how come your skin is getting kinda gooshy?" It's not exactly the question every mom longs to hear. Where was this one going to fit into my thanks program?

Of course, I had to admit, I'd noticed the face thing too. Somewhere around my second annual 39th birthday, it became apparent that I wasn't applying makeup in the same way. Instead of applying, I started to feel I was "filling in the grooves." It became more like "arts and crafts." I'm thankful that I learned to color inside the lines in preschool. (See? I said, "thankful.")

First Thessalonians 5:18 is a giant part of my thanks plan: "give thanks in all circumstances, for this is God's will for you in Christ Jesus." I'm even trying to learn to be thankful in all facial circumstances. I can be thankful, for instance, that my skin, though "gooshier," is much more versatile than it used to be. I'd say it's just about as versatile as my hair. I can wear it up. I can wear it down. Pin it back. Change the color. I can throw it over my shoulder like a Continental soldier. Ah yes, there's something to be said for versatility.

Grace in the Migraine Moments

I'm also thankful for handy-dandy face products. After my son's comment, I decided to try a couple of new exfoliators to "de-goosh." It seemed the logical move: off with the old face, on with the new. The first one I tried didn't do much, so I was forced to use "Exfoliator II," the terrifying sequel. Skin-care tip of the day: When you can't get your hands on Exfoliator II, a brick should work just as well. Falling face first onto a gravel driveway may also do it. This should be followed by extended time reading 1 Thessalonians 5:18.

Would you like an even better tip? This one offers the ultimate makeover. It's from Ephesians 4:22–24: "You were taught, with regard to your former way of life, to put off your old self, which is being corrupted by its deceitful desires; to be made new in the attitude of your minds; and to put on the new self, created to be like God in true righteousness and holiness."

It's sort of like spiritual exfoliation. Scrubbing away that old dead way of life. Sometimes that might be about as pleasant as falling face first onto a gravel driveway. But keeping that old dead way of life is much more painful in the long run. Deceitful desires and old sin habits would have that old self spiraling in a fruitless, defeated, and sorrowful direction.

Thankfully, the Lord doesn't leave us without direction—"face-less." He tells us to take off that old self, then He tells us what we are to put on instead: "put on the new self, created to be like God in true righteousness and holiness" (verse 24). Where should the new self start—the face? Not exactly. Verse 23 says to be "made new in the attitude of your minds." There's no better makeover than to be made more like the Father, putting on righteousness and holiness. When you put on the mind of Christ, His righteousness and holiness are a glorious part of the beauty package. You'll be changed—from head to toe, heart to face. It's like an all-over facial!

As for my face, I've decided I'm okay with a "semigooshy" one outfitted with a few laugh lines. Better to have laughed and lined than never to have laughed at all.

An attitude of gratitude is a powerful thing. A new face? Nah. I'll take a renewed and thankful heart instead, "always giving thanks to God the Father for everything, in the name of our Lord Jesus Christ" (Ephesians 5:20). I think when I'm truly giving thanks in everything, you'll see it written all over my face.

My Face Has Fallen and It Can't Get Up

"Give thanks to the Lord, call on his name;
make known among the nations what he has done.
Sing to him, sing praise to him;
tell of all his wonderful acts.
Glory in his holy name;
let the hearts of those who seek the Lord rejoice.
Look to the Lord and his strength;
seek his face always."

Psalm 105:1–4

part three

Grace for the Everyday Landmines

*Focusing on His plans,
not mine*

chapter eleven

· · · · ·

Deer-ly Departed Plans

I always feel pretty good about myself when I manage to get all five of my kids out the door without misplacing any of them and without anyone going off to school naked. Mornings are wild around my house. After I drop the kids off, though, there's a drive home on a peaceful country road. It's therapeutic.

One morning, deep in "therapy," I mentally mapped out my day. If I timed everything just perfectly, I could get a nagging writing deadline or two resolved, get the house reasonably picked up (at least scrape off the top layer), do enough laundry so I wouldn't have to worry about that naked-kid-thing, and maybe even find something for dinner a pizza guy wouldn't have to deliver.

I was deep into my plans when, without warning, a deer popped out of the woods and right onto the hood of my car! Talk about putting a dent in my plans! Not to mention my car. My radiator was inside my engine!

But the deer fared even worse. An officer arrived a few minutes later and put the poor thing out of its misery. I blubbered like a real idiot. Talk about embarrassing.

I was glad I had already taken the kids to school. I thought they would be even more upset than I was. Of course, when I told them later, my oldest son's first comment was "Cool! Do we get to eat it?" Kids! I pointed out to him that while I had accidentally done the tenderizing, field dressing the thing there in the road had somehow never occurred to me.

Don't let it get around, but I did strut around at church the next evening, bragging to all the guys in my most macho way how I had bagged me a deer. I've got that macho act down. You just pull up your britches a lot, sniff, and wipe your nose with the back of your hand. Then you spit. Okay, I couldn't really bring myself to do the spitting part. Still, they were all deeply impressed.

But guess what happened with all my ambitious plans? Right. Exactly nothing! An hour waiting for a tow truck, more hours at the body shop (though I made the repair man very, very happy), then another few hours chatting with the insurance man. The insurance man was not nearly as happy as the guy at the body shop. As a matter of fact, he mentioned he hoped the deer didn't have any sue-crazy next of kin who might come after me with a wrongful death suit. Anyway, before I knew it, the day was gone.

I should never be so full of my own plans that I forget the Lord might have something completely different in mind. There's no satisfaction in life when I'm wrapped up in my own things—even when everything is deer-free. "The backslider in heart will be filled with his own ways, but a good man will be satisfied from above" (Proverbs 14:14, NKJV). True satisfaction comes from walking with Him every moment.

I want my satisfaction to be in Him wherever I'm walking. Wherever I'm driving, too—if I ever get my car out of the shop.

"For I know the thoughts that I think toward you, says the LORD, thoughts of peace and not of evil, to give you a future and a hope. Then you will call upon Me and go and pray to Me, and I will listen to you. And you will seek Me and find Me, when you search for Me with all your heart."

Jeremiah 29:11–13, NKJV

chapter twelve

It's ... SUPER MOM!

L ook! Up in the sky! It's a bird! It's a plane! ... Oh let's get real. The only place we'll find Super Mom is in the comics—unless, of course, we're talking about that incredible Proverbs 31 superhero, Virtue Woman.

That virtuous woman has long been a wonderful inspiration, a super motivation, and a great frustration for those of us who feel we can't measure up. While the Lord has used her to send me in the right direction more than once, I have to confess to never having actually arrived at the destination. The destination, as you might guess, has been to become Mrs. Proverbs Perfect—Martha Stewart, Mother Teresa, June Cleaver, and Wonder Woman all rolled into one strong, industrious, benevolent lump of creativity.

I should tell you right up front I'm no superhero. It may take me a good half hour just to get my pantyhose untwisted. Some mornings I never do get it right. Those are the days I just take shorter steps. Try to imagine me leaping tall buildings in that kind of pickle. It's not happening in any number of bounds.

If you see an "S" on my shirt, it's most likely a stain and probably means I'm having another bad laundry day. But if I were labeled a heroine, the "S" would have to stand for something more like "Survival Woman"! The basic goal for Survival Woman is to keep my five children in relatively clean underwear (in case they're in an accident), make sure they don't run with any sharp objects, and to raise those children without misplacing any of them.

In my own frustration with the Perfect Woman, I've entertained the circulating rumor she was actually an early alien visitation. The first words written about this Kryptonian ... I mean virtuous ... woman in Proverbs 31:10 are "Who can find a virtuous wife?" (NKJV). And it's hardly a wonder no one can find her—she's out buying fields, making matching red out-fits for her family, and still squeezing in time to run her own home busi-ness. All that, of course, happens after she puts in her gardening and real estate hours. She keeps boldly going … and going … where no battery bunny has gone before.

I personally wanted to focus on the word "maidservants" in verse 15 (NKJV). When I realized I had biblical grounds for a housekeeper, I immedi-ately called "Maidservants-R-Us" to place my order. Then I remembered my microwave, dishwasher, vacuum, and other handy-dandy luxuries, such as running water and preplucked chickens. I had to admit to having a few modern-day maidservants of my own. Painful admission.

Virtue Woman is strong and honorable, wise and kind, loved by hus-band, children, and community. When we look at her in all her glory and feel we don't measure up, we can find ourselves resolving to muster up whatever strength we can to become more like her. Out of guilt we try to organize, sanitize, even computerize ourselves into becoming Virtue Woman.

But verse 25 (NASB) is one of my favorites. It tells us she smiles—some versions even say "laughs"—at the future. Is she running around like a wild woman trying to be like someone else? I don't think so. I think she can laugh because she's resting in what the Lord can do through her. She must know her future rests in His faithful hands. It's a rest that produces obedience, wisdom, kindness, fruitfulness, and contentment to the point of laughter. Just think, if you've learned to rest and laugh, you've already made some progress toward virtue.

What the Lord has for your ministry may not be exactly the same as the Proverbs 31 Woman (you can now breathe a great sigh of relief). You don't have to do everything she does to be successful (another sigh). True virtue is becoming a woman who loves, serves, and honors the Lord.

There is great freedom in understanding that the Lord doesn't wait to love you until you're Super Mom. He loves and accepts you as you are. Striving for perfection in your own strength is what will lead to burnout and major frustration. Frustration—there's my field of expertise. But I can also testify from personal experience that resting in the Lord brings peace, joy, victory, and even laughter.

So let's dedicate ourselves to the Savior. Then the really important works and character qualities will happen a lot more naturally than in our own futile squirming to attain them.

If you honor your God and love your children, then you are Super Mom. And Super Mom still keeps her finger in Proverbs 31. Save the superhero syndrome for the comics.

"Her children rise up and call her blessed;
Her husband also, and he praises her:
'Many daughters have done well,
But you excel them all.'
Charm is deceitful and beauty is passing,
But a woman who fears the LORD, she shall be praised.
Give her of the fruit of her hands,
And let her own works praise her in the gates."

Proverbs 31:28–31, NKJV

chapter thirteen
The Father Nose Best

I t happened several years ago, but I remember it as if it were yesterday. I had been stewing in my hot car all day with my five little ones. I delivered a son to baseball practice, delivered a husband to a church finance meeting, delivered the forgotten ball glove, and a bajillion other deliveries in between. (Who would've thought childbirth would be the easy delivery?)

To top it all off, the day had been packed with one annoying little trauma after another. The ATM ate my card with not so much as a simple acknowledgment—not even a "Thank you, ma'am." Just "INSERT CARD" still blaring at me. The air conditioner in the minivan was suddenly toast (and I don't do that "sweat thing" with grace). All the while, I was having visions—maybe something sort of related to flashbacks—of the past-my-eyeballs mountain of laundry waiting at home for me. (My friend Liz and I like to call it "Mount Washmore.") It had been one of those three-spill dinners, and while there's no use crying over spilled milk, three of them can just about bring anyone to tears. I broke a nail, overspent the budget, and forgot to deliver some clothes to the local clothes closet—yet another delivery hanging over my head—somebody help me!

I was on the verge of shrieking an "Okay! I surrender!" when my daughter Kaley, four years old at the time, interrupted my pity party with the deep thought of the hour: "Mom, how come we gots two holes in our noses?"

A friend gave me the obvious answer later. He said it was so we could still breathe out of one hole when we have a finger in the other.

But since I'm not nearly that quick-thinking, I answered, "Because that's the way God designed us. And we can always know whatever He designs for us is just right."

Grace for the Everyday Landmines

I really hate it when I'm trying to sound wise and motherly to my children and I get conked between the eyes with the jewel of wisdom that's supposed to be for them. Yet there it was—right in my face. I knew the message was for me.

I spoke a prayer of surrender and thanksgiving to the Awesome Designer around a lump in my throat the size of New Jersey.

I'm supposing "I surrender" was precisely the right cry. As I surrendered in trust to His design for my life, all those little annoyances fell right into perspective. And how those tiny annoyances paled into insignificance against the brightness of my countless blessings—five of whom bounced happily in my toasty minivan, breathing through ten perfectly designed nostrils. Praise God for His design.

"Make a joyful shout to the LORD, all you lands!
Serve the LORD with gladness;
Come before His presence with singing.
Know that the LORD, He is God;
It is He who has made us, and not we ourselves;
We are His people and the sheep of His pasture."

Psalm 100:1–3, NKJV

chapter fourteen

·····

Male Order Shopping

A ny other women having trouble buying for men? The last gift-giving occasion, I asked for a list from my husband. I had a tough time reading it. I kept dozing off. I'd share it with you, but I'd run the risk of snoozing through my own book. I'll tell you, though, that the highlight was a paper shredder. I'll provide the list if you're a desperate insomniac. I can help you.

I thought about giving my husband a barbecue grill. Sounds good, right? An excuse to have him do the cooking! But don't expect to have a relaxing evening as he hooks up to the gas line. Men see the imminent danger and get a rush. Women wait by the phone with "9" and "1" predialed. The distinct possibility of living for months with a man who has no eyebrows somehow takes the fun out of the promise of barbecue. No—no grill.

How about tickets to the sporting event du jour? Yeah, that sounds good. But before you rush out to purchase tickets, remember that you might be expected to actually attend the event. Picture watching some team go back and forth until some loud person behind you spills beer on your shoes. I try to have quality conversation with my husband through it all, but I'm amazed when he shows absolutely no interest in the bad accessory choices made by the lady three rows down. "White shoes in this season? And with a brown purse? Pul-lease!" For some reason, he rarely appreciates those gross atrocities, so I'm always willing to be a sport and try a new topic: "Why do you suppose they didn't color coordinate the seats and the walls?" Can you believe my husband would rather watch some game than explore all those possibilities? Nope, not sports, thank you.

A tool is always a good gift choice. Even better, a ladder. But if you give him a tool, he'll try to fix something. If you give him a ladder, he'll want to climb it. "9-1- ..." sound familiar? I'd like to get him something that wouldn't come with the wifely warning, "Be careful, that'll put your eye out."

Gift giving for men has been a problem since the beginning. Eve obviously didn't get it. She gave Adam a used apple. We know where that led.

The good news is that whatever I give my husband, he is always gracious and appreciative—even if it's yet another bottle of aftershave. I don't have to earn his love with gifts. What a relief!

The rest of the good news is that despite Eve's gift and the Fall, I still don't have to earn God's love, either. The Bible says that God loved me long before I was lovable. Me—a sinner—yet Christ died for me! The Bible also tells us that the gift of God is eternal life through Christ. Now there's a gift!

As for my poor husband, looks like it's another tie. Next time I might find something he likes just as well—like a gift certificate for gum surgery or a complimentary upper G.I.

"But God demonstrates his own love for us in this: While we were still sinners, Christ died for us. Since we have now been justified by his blood, how much more shall we be saved from God's wrath through him! For if, when we were God's enemies, we were reconciled to him through the death of his Son, how much more, having been reconciled, shall we be saved through his life!"

Romans 5:8–10

chapter fifteen
· · · · ·
The Meat-Eater and the Need-Meeter

I t's just about time for my baby's 2:00 feeding. He's sixteen. It's amazing how these teens revert to infancy around this age. The feedings are about every two hours. As a matter of fact, I worry about frostbite. His head is only out of the refrigerator for short periods of time. I'm concerned that one of these days an ear could just snap off.

The other day I saw the back of his head in the fridge and said, "Don't eat dinner now. We'll all be eating together in an hour or so."

"This isn't dinner. And don't worry, I'll be hungry in an hour."

Not so. He was hungry again in twenty minutes. And you should've seen the "snack." A can of Spaghettios with meatballs, a sandwich with enough lunch meat on it to feed his entire basketball team, a bowl of cereal, three-quarters of a bag of chips, a half a can of Spam, two glasses of milk and two rows of Oreo cookies. For dinner I should just whip up a side of beef. Of course, it's very possible it could take both sides.

This boy is definitely a carnivore. When I plan the Thanksgiving fixings, I have to ponder exactly how many turkeys it will take. Should I worry I'll cause a run on the market? I'm picturing Andrew going back for another turkey leg—every two hours.

Thankfully, I have a God who meets every need. He meets our real needs, not just the meaty ones. Philippians 4:19 says, "And my God will meet all your needs according to his glorious riches in Christ Jesus."

He is ready and waiting to meet every real need. Of course, sometimes we get a little cloudy on the "real need" issue. Paul mentioned a few verses before, in verses 11–13, "I am not saying this because I am in need, for I have learned to be content whatever the circumstances. I know what it is to be in need, and I know what it is to have plenty. I have learned the secret of being content in any and every situation, whether well fed or hungry, whether living in plenty or in want. I can do everything through him who gives me strength."

When we're depending on the Need-meeter for our strength, we find our needs are surprisingly small. And we can have confidence that when we ask Him to meet those needs, He delights in answering. Earlier in the same chapter of Philippians, Paul wrote, "Do not be anxious about anything, but in everything, by prayer and petition, with thanksgiving, present your requests to God" (verse 6).

That's our charge. Recognize the Need-meeter for whom He really is. Instead of fretting, give the anxious thoughts to God. All those worries— even concerns of snapping ears and turkey futures. And be thankful.

Who meets our real needs? Our Heavenly Father. Every two hours. Every hour. Every millisecond.

"He who regards one day as special, does so to the Lord. He who eats meat, eats to the Lord, for he gives thanks to God; and he who abstains, does so to the Lord and gives thanks to God. For none of us lives to himself alone and none of us dies to himself alone. If we live, we live to the Lord; and if we die, we die to the Lord. So, whether we live or die, we belong to the Lord."

Romans 14:6–8

part four

Grace for Spiritual Clorox

*Focusing on a
continuous sin clean-up*

chapter sixteen

· · · · ·

Sale On!

H ave you ever noticed that when moms shop, they rarely get to shop for themselves? Let me clarify: They don't get to buy for themselves—not without a truckload of guilt anyway. If you're a mom, you know the routine. You find something you want. You decide it's too great a deal to pass up. You take it for several laps around the store. Then you put it back and get something for your kids.

But my shopping venture of a few weeks ago didn't go that way. I was walking by the ladies' clothing section when a cute sweater-vest caught my eye. It was wonderfully bright and perky with some subtle flowers here and there. I didn't really need another sweater vest, you understand, but I wanted it. I stood studying it for a few minutes—just to truly appreciate it. Then came the clincher. Those three little words all women long to hear: On Sale Now!

It was sort of like I was walking along, minding my own business, when WHAM! this lovely yet vicious sweater-vest attacked me and forced itself into my hands. Next thing I knew, the sweater had made it three laps around the store, through the cashier, and I was wearing it.

As I read Psalm 1 the next day, it occurred to me it's pretty much the same with sin. "Blessed is the man who walks not in the counsel of the ungodly, nor stands in the path of sinners, nor sits in the seat of the scornful; but his delight is in the law of the LORD, and in His law he meditates day and night" (verses 1–2, NKJV). And verse 6 says: "For the LORD knows the way of the righteous, but the way of the ungodly shall perish" (NKJV).

At first, we're just passing by, walking past the ungodly. Maybe we're catching a glimpse of something on TV or hearing something inappropriate at the office. Or maybe it's a thought that flies into our minds unexpectedly. Suddenly we find ourselves standing and listening to that thought or that counsel—sort of like people stop to just peek at a train wreck. The next thing we know, the sin is ours. We're sitting in the middle of it—wearing it, if you will. We may think we were the victims of an attack, but we've actually made a choice to buy into the sin and "put it on."

As for the sweater-vest, I proudly put it on the next day. Daniel, my five-year-old, said, "Mom! I like your new vest!" I smiled one of those "I'm so pleased with myself" smiles as he went on to share what I'm sure he considered the ultimate compliment: "Mom, you look just like the ladies who work at Kmart!" I looked down at my bright vest. He was right—it did look like a store uniform.

The moral: Keep on walking. Keep your face in the Word and you won't find yourself sitting in the middle of the perishing sinners. And if you'd like a brightly colored sweater-vest, keep me in mind. I'm having a blue-light special in the sweater section of my closet.

"But his delight is in the law of the LORD,
And in His law he meditates day and night.
He shall be like a tree planted by the rivers of water,
That brings forth its fruit in its season,
Whose leaf also shall not wither;
And whatever he does shall prosper. ...
For the LORD knows the way of the righteous,
But the way of the ungodly shall perish."

Psalm 1:2–3, 6, NKJV

chapter seventeen
. . . . .
Anger Is All the Rage

H ave you noticed anger seems to be in fashion in some spheres? I've even heard sports figures brag they "get up" for the game by fueling their anger. (For pete's sake, why don't they just go out and rent a teenager?)

Kids in general often know exactly how to find our anger buttons, don't they? And then they jump up and down on them. It's almost always the little things that make us crazy. It's easiest for me, for example, to lose my cool when we're running late. For the record, that's an everyday anger test. It seems that the morning the alarm doesn't go off and the dryer is on the fritz, the kids shift into some sort of alternate time reality. It's like a bad "Twilight Zone" episode—and it's exasperating.

We were having "one of those mornings," and I was barking out orders left and right when I noticed one of my children just standing in the kitchen staring at the orange juice can. "Just standing" is the cardinal sin on a late morning. I asked, "Why in the world are you just standing and staring when you don't even have your jeans on?" The answer: "Mom, it says, 'Concentrate.'"

It's not only the tardy challenge. I could spend this entire chapter ranting about the anger challenges of laundry. Washing an ink pen in the load with your favorite outfit can get you worked up into a pretty good lather, can't it? It's even worse when you wash a piece of bubble gum and it makes it all the way through the dryer. Static cling is the least of our worries. I probably don't even need to mention the tissue-in-the-pocket laundry disaster. That's a weekly happening at my house. We're Baptists, but we're trying to give it up for "lint."

It's not always just the kids pushing our anger buttons. Have you ever hung drapes with your spouse? How about wallpaper? How about simply watching your spouse hang drapes or wallpaper?

Grace for Spiritual Clorox

I hate the way anger turns me into a crab. And it inspires all kinds of self-ishness. It's usually about my imaginary rights being violated—selfishness to the max. That's what inspired me to come up with the anger/crabbiness/self-ishness crustacean line of the year: "When you're crabby, it's easy to be a little shellfish." (Get it?)

There is a righteous anger, but few of us experience that one. Let's face it, ours is almost always of the selfish variety. And what does anger really pro-duce? The fastest time at the swim meet? One less tardy at school? Maybe, but at what cost? While swimming the fastest time and having the best on-time record at school, we're spewing meanness and crabbiness. Ephesians 4:31–32 says, "Get rid of all bitterness, rage and anger, brawling and slander, along with every form of malice. Be kind and compassionate to one another, forgiving each other, just as in Christ God forgave you." Get rid of it—put it away. Put away anger and the like—just as we "put away" the lint-covered laundry. Oh, wait … Lord, have mercy and let me do a better job putting away anger than I do putting away laundry. Can you picture mountains of anger piled up in large plastic baskets in every room in the house? There would be a brawl for sure.

We're told to put away the bitterness and anger, but we're not left wonder-ing what should replace it. Put away the angry things and, according to verse 32, put on kindness, tenderheartedness, and forgiveness, with our Heavenly Father as our example.

Learning what to put away and what to put on can help you keep your cool when you discover the kids have been playing deep-sea diver in your aquari-um—with the cat. Even if you happen to find your six year old's broccoli from last week under the cover of your hot rollers, you can look to the Lord and find the strength to get rid of anger and put on a tender heart. Anger is not the moti-vational tool it's cracked up to be in the world. You'll find greater reward doing it the Jesus way, showing compassion and forgiveness—even if you didn't make the broccoli discovery until after you plugged in the rollers.

"But now you yourselves are to put off all these: anger, wrath, malice, blas-phemy, filthy language out of your mouth. Do not lie to one another, since you have put off the old man with his deeds, and have put on the new man who is renewed in knowledge according to the image of Him who created him."

Colossians 3:8–10, NKJV

chapter eighteen
· · · · ·

Move Out!

M ove out" takes on a truly military tone when seven years' worth of junk has to be stuffed into seven thousand cardboard boxes. Factor in my five pack-rat kids and you understand these were no ordinary moving maneuvers. I wondered how on earth I could relocate without a backhoe. This was a major battle.

You should've seen me on packing day. I paced back and forth in front of the ladies who had come to help. I was the commander, readying the troops. My feather duster was tucked under my arm like a riding crop as I began my moving address: "I'd like to thank you for signing on for this mission. Some of you might find yourselves waning in the heat of the battle. Others may discover new courage. And some of you … (sniff) … might not be coming home."

Okay, that was for drama. They all made it home. Not without battle scars, however. It was frightening; I didn't have mere dust bunnies on top of my china cabinet. These things looked more like fuzzy buffaloes.

Thankfully, I had provided the women with some basic training. I decided I could desensitize them before they got to the house by taking them for a ride in my minivan. On the way to my buffalo-filled home, one asked, "Is this a pickle in the cup holder?"

"My kids don't eat pickles. I think that's a hotdog from last baseball season." She had to go home right after she regained consciousness. The rest of the ladies were fine after they put their heads between their knees. Still, I couldn't bring myself to make them look in the glove compartment. I think the Geneva Convention has rules against such atrocities.

Several were overcome during the chemical warfare phase of the moving battle. It's a common result of mixing the chemicals needed to fight dust buffaloes with the ones needed for that scum that gathers over the stove. They're recovering. The therapy for post-packing trauma syndrome (PPTS) is also help-

Grace for Spiritual Clorox

ing. Thankfully, the flashbacks are starting to subside.

There was a particularly perilous moment in the kitchen, however, when one of the ladies made a gruesome discovery. It was a potato that had fallen behind a pile of junk in one of the cabinets. But it was no longer legally a pota-to. It looked like a brown, raisiney grenade. We were all distressed when we discovered the local bomb squad doesn't respond to potatoes.

I was amazed no one in my family had ever gotten a whiff of the rotting potato/grenade. We never had even a hint it was back there shriveling. Believe it or not, there wasn't even any mold on the little sucker. I guess it's still not surprising not one of the packing ladies wanted to touch the thing. But before we could move, the dead spud had to go.

In the same way, isn't it amazing the spiritual dirt we can have hidden away? Little things can be rotting—shriveling right under our noses—and we don't so much as catch a whiff. It's a spiritual battle and the enemy is ever ready to lob his bombs. He loves to see us rendered fruitless. Sometimes he schemes a sneak attack. It's not the kind of attack that immediately blows up in our faces, but rather an undercover mission where the enemy secures hidden places of rottenness that quietly shrivel our spirits.

Romans 6:13 says, "Do not offer the parts of your body to sin, as instruments of wickedness, but rather offer yourselves to God, as those who have been brought from death to life." We can ignore those pockets of disobedience we've tucked away, or we can offer every part of ourselves to God. Before we can move to a closer walk with Him, we shouldn't be surprised if He pulls out that "sin potato" and says, "We really have to take care of this before we can move on."

I've now moved into a clean, new home—completely free of shriveled potatoes. When we allow the Father to cleanse us from sneaky rottenness, we can enjoy the same kind of clean, sweet closeness with him.

So go ahead. Plan a spiritual military action of your own. Execute Recon Plan "Tossoutthepotato!" Ready? Move out!

"Therefore, since Christ suffered for us in the flesh, arm yourselves also with the same mind, for he who has suffered in the flesh has ceased from sin, that he no longer should live the rest of his time in the flesh for the lusts of men, but for the will of God."

1 Peter 4:1–2, NKJV

chapter nineteen
· · · · ·
The Truth and Nothing but the Truth

I s there anything more heartwarming than listening to your toddler tell you the truth even when he knows he's going to get in trouble for it?

"Did you eat that cookie after I told you not to?"

"Uh huh. Me like cookies." There's something rather comforting about an honest, chocolate-lipped answer from your own little Cookie Monster.

The first heartbreak begins when you realize that the only reason he told you the truth was that he hadn't figured out how to lie yet. The second heartbreak happens when he actually does figure out how to lie.

My parents still managed to laugh at my brother's first attempt as a pre-school liar. My folks had told him not to play on the creaky fence in the backyard. Randy played on it anyway and (surprise, surprise) it came crashing down. When my dad asked what had happened to it, Randy told him that a herd of buffalo came through the backyard and trampled it.

Buffalo? Surely even a three-year-old knew that we blamed everything on the Cold War back then. He could've said it was a herd of Russians—my parents might've bought that one. Better yet, if he had creatively made a link between fences, social barriers, and learning to tear down walls, the whole family might've had a warm, fuzzy moment. I can picture us joining hands with our parents and singing "Kum-bah-yah."

But somehow they knew he was lying. Parents are quick like that. He didn't get away with that one. Through the years, Randy either learned not to lie or he got better at it—I'm not sure which.

Grace for Spiritual Clorox

Our world seems to propagate a natural and polished ability to lie. We have a proven record of lying—from the most powerful world leaders right on down the line. Even family TV shows are full of lies and deception. Lots of them never present lying as a wrong choice. How many times did Andy lie to Aunt Bea? Even Andy! Even watching "The Andy Griffith Show" is a learning experience: Lying 101.

Growing up in that kind of school, the chances are pretty remote that we'll automatically learn the right lessons about the value of truth. But Ephesians 4:15 says, "Instead, speaking the truth in love, we will in all things grow up into him who is the Head, that is, Christ." If we do our growing up in Christ, making Jesus the boss of our tongues, speaking the truth can become a natural part of living for him.

Instead of excusing lies by putting them in little categories according to size, shape, and color, we can head down the road to maturity by listening to what God's Word says. Is "a little white lie" as bad as one of those big whoppers? Our Heavenly Father doesn't mince words: " 'These are the things you are to do: Speak the truth to each other, and render true and sound judgment in your courts; do not plot evil against your neighbor, and do not love to swear falsely. I hate all this,' declares the Lord" (Zechariah 8:16–17).

A lie is a lie in God's Book—and He hates lies. Lying is part of the old, destructive way of life. Colossians 3:9–10 gives us clear instruction for our new life: "Do not lie to each other, since you have taken off your old self with its practices and have put on the new self, which is being renewed in knowledge in the image of its Creator."

There is great value in the truth. It's unspeakably precious. It's even freeing. What we do with the truth will teach our children. We either teach them to tell the truth by our good example, or we teach them by our poor example that lying is no big deal.

I want to perpetuate truth in my home—the truth, the whole truth, and nothing but the truth. So help me, God.

And He will help. He delights in truth. Scripture says, "The Lord detests lying lips, but he delights in men who are truthful" (Proverbs 12:22). With His direction and by the in-filling power of His Holy Spirit, truth is a way of life. And my God is all-powerful. More powerful than a herd of stampeding buffalo.

The Truth and Nothing but the Truth

"So Jesus said, 'When you have lifted up the Son of Man, then you will know that I am the one I claim to be and that I do nothing on my own but speak just what the Father has taught me. The one who sent me is with me; he has not left me alone, for I always do what pleases him.' Even as he spoke, many put their faith in him.

"To the Jews who had believed him, Jesus said, 'If you hold to my teaching, you are really my disciples. Then you will know the truth, and the truth will set you free.'"

John 8:28–32

chapter twenty
· · · · ·
The Cover-Up

Something was wrong at school. Very wrong. It was only the bravery of my oldest son that finally brought resolution. Of course, it was that same son who actually caused the situation in the first place. Nevertheless, he snapped into action, mustered up no small amount of courage, and, yes, he CLEANED OUT HIS LOCKER!

People teared up as they walked by. It wasn't emotion over his bravery. It was some sort of gray fog that was looming over the locker. The stench was causing the paint to peel.

The cleaning process was an adventure—maybe it was more of an excavation. No, excavation isn't a strong enough word either. It was more like a hostile confrontation. He might have been better prepared for the battle if it were a military school locker. Still, I think we'd all be pretty amazed, if not thoroughly grossed out, at the spoils of war a ninth grader can acquire when he resolves to clean his locker. "So there's that government report." "Who put Ben-Gay in here?" "Hey, I remember when these shoes fit!"

Andrew continued the onslaught on his locker until he finally sniffed out the enemy. He found it sandwiched between a couple of stiff, brown socks (hey—wait a minute—I only buy him white socks). It was one of those frozen pocket sandwiches. Needless to say, it was no longer frozen. It's safe to say that it was no longer a sandwich either. It was green and purple and slimy—the part that was still there, that is. Half of it was gone—even though he hadn't ever eaten any of it. It just sort of disintegrated into that mysterious place where disgusting things go when they die. The rest of it was still alive, but definitely injured.

Once he peeled away the socks, the stench moved the battle into more of a chemical-warfare mode. Even after Andrew hauled off the slime pocket, the stench didn't seem to understand that its instigator was gone. The gray fog still loomed. So Andrew fought the chemical battle the way most ninth-grade guys fight the battle of the stench. He poured half a bottle of cologne in his locker. He ended up with a different battle—something like Mold-zilla meets High Karate Kid.

Isn't that how we treat our sin sometimes? We ignore it until it just won't be ignored anymore. And then we try to cover it over by "over-cologning" it. We excuse it as a little boo-boo, an error in judgment, or "just part of my personality." What we really need to do is recognize that stench for what it is: sin. Then we need to hose out the locker of our lives and start fresh.

Jesus is the only one who can clean up the stench. "If we confess our sins, he is faithful and just and will forgive us our sins and purify us from all unrighteousness." (1 John 1:9) Yes, He can purify even the stuff we've left growing all semester.

Covering over our sin gets us nowhere. Proverbs 28:13 says, "He who conceals his sins does not prosper, but whoever confesses and renounces them finds mercy."

He finds mercy. In some analogies, he may even find a science project.

"For if by the one man's offense death reigned through the one, much more those who receive abundance of grace and of the gift of righteous-ness will reign in life through the One, Jesus Christ. Therefore, as through one man's offense judgment came to all men, resulting in con-demnation, even so through one Man's righteous act the free gift came to all men, resulting in justification of life. For as by one man's disobe-dience many were made sinners, so also by one Man's obedience many will be made righteous. Moreover the law entered that the offense might abound. But where sin abounded, grace abounded much more, so that as sin reigned in death, even so grace might reign through righteous-ness to eternal life through Jesus Christ our Lord."

Romans 5:17–21, NKJV

part five

Grace for Head Scratchers

Focusing on the Lord through the tough questions

chapter twenty-one
·····
Socks, Cellulite, and Other Mysteries

L ife is full of questions and mysteries. What is the meaning of life? Why do our socks periodically "rapture" and why don't they ever go up in pairs? Why can only one person in the house put on a new roll of toilet paper? Why do we still get cellulite when we're not eating anything fun?

If any of these mysteries are plaguing you, here are some insights and tidbits of wisdom to offer you some help: Check your Bible for the meaning of life. Buy all black socks in only one style. Get the mega-quadruple rolls of t.p. and then consider a toilet-paper alarm-system. Instead of vacationing at the beach, go to the mountains where cellulite doesn't matter.

Many of the mysteries of life are beyond explanation, such as how those fuzz balls get inside the lining of our jackets and why women always go to the ladies' room in pairs. But we have been entrusted with the knowledge of the greatest mystery of all. Jesus said in Mark 4:11, "To you it has been given to know the mystery of the kingdom of God" (NKJV). Jesus set up His kingdom in our hearts when He came and gave His life on the cross.

Mismatched socks, cellulite, and fuzz balls are still a part of this mysterious fallen world. And personally, I'm still further baffled by the way my kids can't hear me yell that it's cleanup time, and yet they can hear me unwrap a Ding Dong from two blocks away. But if we're talking about the truly important issues in life, we don't have to find ourselves baffled. (And it's yet another mystery why it's so tough for me to put Ding Dongs and other vital forms of chocolate in the category of those things that are less important.)

Grace for Head Scratchers

Ephesians 1:7–9 says: "In Him we have redemption through His blood, the forgiveness of sins, according to the riches of His grace which He made to abound toward us in all wisdom and prudence, having made known to us the mystery of His will, according to His good pleasure which He purposed in Himself" (NKJV). He has made known to us the mystery of His will! What a blessing that in a world of questions we've been given some concrete answers in God's Word about the things that really count.

Who put the grilled-cheese sandwich in the VCR? That one will have to remain a mystery.

"In Him we have redemption through His blood, the forgiveness of sins, according to the riches of His grace which He made to abound toward us in all wisdom and prudence, having made known to us the mystery of His will, according to His good pleasure which He purposed in Himself, that in the dispensation of the fullness of the times He might gather together in one all things in Christ, both which are in heaven and which are on earth—in Him. In Him also we have obtained an inheritance, being predestined according to the purpose of Him who works all things according to the counsel of His will, that we who first trusted in Christ should be to the praise of His glory."

Ephesians 1:7–12, NKJV

chapter twenty-two
·····
Will There Be Chocolate in Heaven?

W on't it be great to have all of our questions answered when we get to "Glory Land"? Like the lyrics in that old favorite hymn, "We'll understand it better by and by." I have some biggies, not the least of which might be "Why didn't chocolate get its own day of creation?" Can't you imagine a thunderous, "Let there be chocolate!" (Needless to say, it would be good.)

There are still those other plaguing questions: "Why do babies especially love to barf on 'dry clean only' clothes?" "Why is it kids can never smell wet towels fermenting in the corners of their rooms?" "How do you divide one cereal box toy among three kids?"

I'll bet we'll have all those answers and more. And we'll finally be able to program the VCR—although we won't need to anymore. We'll figure out how to work that thigh-blaster thing—although we won't need that anymore, either. Hey, that is heaven!

I'm also looking forward to asking questions of famous Bible personalities. Well, my chat with Eve will probably be more of a lecture. But I love the fact we'll be able to rub elbows with Abraham, Isaac, and Jacob—and we won't have to worry about running into any of those evil factions such as the Amorites, the Canaanites, or the *Cellulites*. Nope, no evil allowed.

The blessing works both ways. There are questions we hear on earth we won't hear in heaven: "Do you own your own home and could I interest you in vinyl siding?" "Could I run a copy of your insurance card?" "Paper or plastic?" "Can I put that on your charge?" "Smoking or nonsmoking?" "Would you like to see a dessert menu?" Actually, we may still hear the dessert question, but I'm thinking surely the smoking one will be history.

I love thinking of heaven. No broken shoelaces. No traffic jams. No bad-hair days. No low-fat, low-carb, low-taste diets. We won't need to worry about forming teams to deal with the Y3K problem. Y4K won't be a problem either. In fact, we won't have to deal with time anymore at all. That means I'll never be late again. Who can imagine that?

Since it will be timeless there, do you suppose we'll be able to get snapshots of the great happenings of history? Imagine asking to see that parting of the Red Sea scene one more time just so we can have another photo op. This is going to make a great scrapbook page!

The Book of Revelation gives us little glimpses of the wonder of heaven. Imagine no more pain, no more night, no more wickedness. Thinking of that future blissful, beautiful, peaceful, problem-free life in heaven helps us remember all the broken shoelaces of this life are temporary. This is not our real home. We have a living hope that keeps reminding our hearts that streets of gold are right around the corner. It's a corner that will take us straight into the presence of Jesus.

How glorious that we can head into His presence secure in the future He's mapped out for us. First Peter 1:3–4 reminds us, "Praise be to the God and Father of our Lord Jesus Christ! In his great mercy he has given us new birth into a living hope through the resurrection of Jesus Christ from the dead, and into an inheritance that can never perish, spoil or fade—kept in heaven for you."

Our future hope is "sealed and burped" in a sort of holy Tupperware of the Lord's design. Our inheritance is kept nice and fresh for us where it can't perish or spoil. Just as our trust in the risen Lord is a safe trust, our hope in Him is a safe hope. We can know all of our questions will be answered someday. Those questions can't dim our bright hope one little bit.

For the record, I do know there will be chocolate in heaven. Revelation 7:17 says there will be no more tears. That cinches it for me.

It's healthy to enjoy thoughts of heaven. Picturing yourself sitting at the feet of Jesus can lift your heart and put a spring in your step in the here and now—even if you're having one of those "broken shoelace/floppy shoe" days. You can joyfully keep on walking knowing that Jesus is the One who will make heaven, well … heaven!

So go ahead and envision your glorious future with Jesus. Those thoughts are sweeter than a chocolate dessert buffet—and without the cellulite!

"And there shall be no more curse, but the throne of God and of the Lamb shall be in it, and His servants shall serve Him. They shall see His face, and His name shall be on their foreheads. There shall be no night there: They need no lamp nor light of the sun, for the Lord God gives them light. And they shall reign forever and ever."

Revelation 22:3–5, NKJV

chapter twenty-three

· · · · ·

Camp
Trust-a-Lot

I am a city girl. I think I could've been born in the middle of the woods and I would still have to classify myself as a city girl. I've never felt that need to "enjoy nature"—never really longed for the great outdoors. I think I do have a great sense of adventure. It's just that it's for indoor adventure. I enjoy a nice tree as much as anyone, but isn't that why God made picture windows? And for every tree, there are a zillion bugs. That pretty much ruins it for me even before we talk about the sweat factor.

My family and I have a nice home. We pay money for this nice home, and then we pay more to fill it with every convenience. Camping, as I see it, is leaving this nice home (while still paying for it) and leaving all my conveniences, to go to a place that has exactly zero conveniences. Then you pay the campground for the lack of conveniences. Does anyone else see a sad irony here?

Awhile back, I reluctantly agreed to go camping with my family. I can't over-emphasize the word "reluctantly." You can still see the fingernail marks from my house (with all the conveniences) to the hot, bug-infested campground.

We happened to be there on the hottest weekend of the millennium—somewhere around 147 degrees. My five children, my husband, and I squished our sweaty bodies into the three-man tent. Did I mention the 147-degree temperature? How about the buzzard-size mosquitoes that threatened to carry off my children? Did I mention those? I fought off the urge to mumble, "Are we having fun yet?"

My husband, ever the indoor/outdoor adventurer, suggested that we sit in a sweaty family circle and tell our favorite Bible story. When it was my turn, all I could think of was the Children of Israel wandering in the wilderness. They were forced to camp in tents for forty years. It was stern PUNISHMENT for their sinful rebellion toward God. My husband and children were all deeply moved by my heartfelt sharing.

As I lay there trying not to think about bugs, snakes, and assorted disgusting and/or frightening members of the bio-network, I do remember clicking my heels together with a "There's no place like home." But when I opened my eyes, I was still there—up to my eyeballs in bugs and swimming in a sea of sweat.

It's amazing how camping forces people to think Godward. Some out of awe for the beauty of nature. Others out of fear of those bio-network members. Either way, we can trust in an all-powerful Creator, knowing that He is always perfectly able to care for us and that He has a plan. He had a plan for Jonah even in the belly of the big fish. He had a plan for the Children of Israel even as they wandered in the wilderness and camped in smoldering tents for forty years. I knew he had a plan for my life—even when I was whining about my own wilderness experience (Get it, "wilderness" experience!). And even while I was camping, I really always knew that whatever the circumstances, His arms were strong enough to keep me in the center of His plan for me.

Psalm 9:9 tells us that the Lord is "a refuge for the oppressed, a stronghold in times of trouble." He is our refuge, our safe place, our "convenience-filled home," if you will, when we've been oppressed. How comforting to know that He is our stronghold in every situation and that He is trustworthy through every trial. The next verse says, "Those who know your name will trust in you, for you, Lord, have never forsaken those who seek you." Anyone who really knows the Father by name knows that He is trustworthy. He never forsakes His children who truly seek Him.

I didn't have to seek the Lord very long the morning after our night of camping before I was delivered. My husband is a merciful man, so we left the campground early—before I had time to complain about more than fifty or sixty inconveniences. On the way home (to all our wonderful and even more deeply appreciated conveniences), I could hardly contain my joy. Revival almost broke out in the car.

Through mosquito peril, overworked sweat glands—even every real danger—we can trust in our faithful Father. "Trust in him at all times, O people; pour out your hearts to him, for God is our refuge" (Psalm 62:8). Praise God for the safety we find in Him. Even sailing on Sweat Sea.

"The Lord also will be a refuge for the oppressed,
A refuge in times of trouble.
And those who know Your name will put their trust in You;
For You, Lord, have not forsaken those who seek You.
Sing praises to the Lord, who dwells in Zion!
Declare His deeds among the people."

Psalm 9:9–11, NKJV

chapter twenty-four

. . . . .

www.savvythis .com

My kids don't know that people once played solitaire with real cards. When they were teaching me to play computer pinball, they laughed at me when I pounded the enter key to get the ball to go faster. Of course, I laughed right back when I caught one leaning into the turns on his imaginary racetrack.

The computer is a big part of our kids' lives. They love the games, they can pick up school assignments and schedules, and a research paper is just a couple of clicks away. (One of my kids finally had to write a paper by hand the other day. He asked me how to do a manual spell check.)

Me? Sure, I know my way around the computer. Never mind that the information I've garnered in the past decade my kids picked up in one semester—of THIRD GRADE. It took me longer than that to figure out that a "screen" saver wouldn't necessarily keep bugs out of my Windows. I also had to nix that pesky habit of fixing typos with correction fluid on the monitor.

And my computer savvy has caused a bit (or byte) of confusion around the house. How many times now have I tried to reboot the microwave? My dishwasher hasn't yet completely recovered from that last defragging. I've even tried to enter my password on the TV. Artificial intelligence? I could still use the all-natural kind.

I have to admit that I would miss life without the computer. I'm picturing my children blinking dazedly at me with every homework assignment. And what if I couldn't check their Web sites to find out what's going on their lives? I think I'd even miss the spam. Life without warm fuzzy stories and goofy jokes? No promises of gift certificates or scrolling pictures? No warnings of bad luck if certain slices of spam aren't forwarded to forty-seven people within three minutes? Thanks, Bill Gates.

I may not know everything about computers, but I know enough to know that computers don't know everything. As a matter of fact, they only know what we tell them to know. I also know enough to know that I know the most important thing to know. You know? Ephesians 3:17–19 says, "that Christ may dwell in your hearts through faith; that you, being rooted and grounded in love, may be able ... to know the love of Christ which passes knowledge" (NKJV).

Being "in the know" in the one and only important way is knowing the love of Christ. Jesus is the One who has put us "in the know," and He's given us a knowing that "passes knowledge." You can't find a better knowledge in this world. Put that in your computer and forward it.

I'll leave you with two computer tips for the day:

1. Don't get so wrapped up in any form of earthly/computer knowledge that you forget that real knowing is knowing Jesus, and

2. Never try to roll up your Windows.

If you need more information, you'll have to wait for me to download it. Excuse me while I go ask my second grader how to do that.

"My son, if you accept my words
and store up my commands within you,
turning your ear to wisdom
and applying your heart to understanding,
and if you call out for insight
and cry aloud for understanding,
and if you look for it as for silver
and search for it as for hidden treasure,
then you will understand the fear of the Lord
and find the knowledge of God.
For the Lord gives wisdom,
and from his mouth come knowledge and understanding."

Proverbs 2:1–6

chapter twenty-five
·····
The Grass Is Always Greener?

I was so excited when I found out our new house would have a mudroom. It took on new meaning as we tried to get our lawn started. For the seed to germinate, the sprinklers had to be going almost nonstop. That, however, makes the lawn a massive mud pit. Every time my husband went out to move the sprinklers, he sunk into the "lawn" to near ankle-level. I wonder how many shoes he lost? I could usually tell when he was coming in by that "schlur-urp" sound he made when he pulled his feet out of the pit. More than once he came through the mudroom looking like something from "It Came from Sludge Lagoon."

I was disturbed that my mudroom was evidently confused as to its purpose. All that mud was supposed to stay in the mudroom, right? Isn't that how it got its name? So why was I finding sludge all over my new carpet?

As for growing the grass, I think childbirth was easier. As a matter of fact, at the first sign of baby grass, my husband did everything just short of passing out candy cigars. I have to admit, I was thrilled too. Not so much because I have any kind of decent concern about the grass. I was rejoicing because I had the promise of a sludge-free mudroom.

My husband's rejoicing was definitely different from mine. It was more of a Psalm 147:7–8 kind of rejoicing: "Sing to the Lord with thanksgiving; make music to our God on the harp. He covers the sky with clouds; he supplies the earth with rain and makes grass grow on the hills." As you might imagine, the neighbors did gawk a bit as he played his harp to the Lord who makes the grass grow. That's okay. We had to find a way to break in our new neighbors anyway.

Seeding, however, was not all there was to grass-growing. We seeded. Then reseeded. Then re-reseeded. We're planning to re-re-reseed soon. I'm sure the birds will congregate at our place once again with their little bibs and trays. They're thinking we're setting out yet another birdie buffet. There goes the seed.

And since we're talking about perishable seed, I have to mention that the Bible does, too. Spiritually speaking, there is a perishable seed and an imperishable seed. First Peter 1:23–25 says, "For you have been born again, not of perishable seed, but of imperishable, through the living and enduring word of God. For, 'All men are like grass, and all their glory is like the flowers of the field; the grass withers and the flowers fall, but the word of the Lord stands forever.'"

God tells me in His Word that I've been born again from that imperishable kind of seed. It's dependable—unlike that wimpy, withering grass seed that's here today, bird-food tomorrow. His promise is living and enduring.

Not the lawn. Like the glory of man, I'm afraid it's still pretty wimpy. That's okay. I don't have time to spend on it anyway—now that I have to regularly mow the mudroom.

"Praise the Lord.
How good it is to sing praises to our God,
  how pleasant and fitting to praise him!
The Lord builds up Jerusalem;
  he gathers the exiles of Israel.
He heals the brokenhearted
  and binds up their wounds.
He determines the number of the stars
  and calls them each by name.
Great is our Lord and mighty in power;
  his understanding has no limit.
The Lord sustains the humble
  but casts the wicked to the ground.
Sing to the Lord with thanksgiving;
  make music to our God on the harp.
He covers the sky with clouds;
  he supplies the earth with rain
  and makes grass grow on the hills."

Psalm 147:1–8

part six

Grace to Love Without Bellyaching

*Focusing on loving others
no matter what*

chapter twenty-six

· · · · ·

A Friendly Reminder

F riendships are a must for women. If it weren't for friends, women would have to go to the ladies' room alone. And who would offer a truthful assessment about whether an outfit makes your hips look big?

I have a Mustache Pact with my closest friends. If any one of us goes into a coma, the others are honor bound by our pact to come and wax the mustache of the comatose friend. We women love to share those special moments.

I shared another special moment with friends recently. Several of us were hurrying to a surprise baby shower. We were hurrying because it's tough to surprise the guest of honor when she gets to the party before the guests.

We had pooled our resources to buy "the stroller to end all strollers." It was a collapsible stroller that would stroll the baby, carry the baby, swing the baby—maybe even change the baby—I'm not sure. It was Stroller-ama!

I told the others to run in while I got Super Stroller. I jerked it into position and started sprinting. Unfortunately, about mid-driveway, Stroller-zilla realized I hadn't fully locked it into place (emphasis on the aforementioned collapsible feature). It collapsed neatly into storage mode.

I probably don't need to give you a science lesson on "momentum," but let me mention I had a lot of it working for me. The fact the Stroller-nator stopped on a dime didn't mean much to my little sprinting body, which was immediately airborne.

Maybe you don't know me personally and think me ungraceful.

Grace to Love Without Bellyaching

Granted, you probably wouldn't want me to transport subatomic particles on a regular basis, but I don't want you to forever imagine me as a klutz. So maybe it would be better if you could please picture a graceful triple axel jump over the top of the stroller with sort of a one-point landing. I finished it off with a lovely flat-on-the-back pose, staring up at the sky for effect. I'd give it a 6.9.

Thankfully, I had my wonderful friends there to rush over and make sure I was okay. Of course, they couldn't actually ask me if I was all right since those dear friends were laughing so hard they were about to damage some internal organs! One of them couldn't even stay. She made a beeline for the house. You know what can happen to laughing mothers.

That's another thing we love to share: laughter.

This is a little reminder. If it's been awhile since you've made time for friends, take the time and share a laugh with a sister. We need each other. There are certain things, concepts, even certain words, only women understand. "Mauve" and "taupe" are a couple of good examples.

Call up your special bud today. While you have her on the line, you might also want to take care of that coma/mustache thing.

"Two are better than one,
Because they have a good reward for their labor.
For if they fall, one will lift up his companion.
But woe to him who is alone when he falls,
For he has no one to help him up.
Again, if two lie down together, they will keep warm;
But how can one be warm alone?
Though one may be overpowered by another, two can withstand him.
And a threefold cord is not quickly broken."

Ecclesiastes 4:9–12, NKJV

chapter twenty-seven
· · · · ·

Labor Negotiations

I this your first baby?" "Is this your last?" "When are you due?" "Are you sure you're not having a litter?" "Did I ever tell you about my niney-three-hour labor?" By my fifth baby, I'd heard them all. Everyone seems to have something to say to a pregnant woman. Some comments are sweet. Some thoughtful. Some incredibly annoying. One of my favorites was "You look like you're about to pop." That one was surely the most ridiculous. I was not about to pop. I was about to mom.

I've almost always been five feet tall. My babies were eight- and nine-pounders. How many pounds of baby do you suppose that would be per square inch of me? You can try the math if you like, but let me just save you the trouble and tell you that I really did look like I was having a litter. I had baby busting out from my armpits to my knees. But when those wild pregnancy hormones kick in, the last thing a mom-to-be wants to hear is how she really looks (if she looks like I did). No wait, the last thing she wants to hear is how much weight she SHOULD'VE gained. My doctor told me I should gain about twenty pounds. I'm a goal-oriented person. I was very proud when I had reached my goal before I even reached my second trimester.

The Bible says that the fruit of the womb (not to be confused with any particular brand of underwear) is a reward. Maybe there are a few times we've been known to mutter through clenched teeth, "What did I ever do to deserve this … reward?" Still, I've never known even one woman who didn't find motherhood more rewarding than she ever imagined. I can't imagine life without my five sweet rewards.

Grace to Love Without Bellyaching

If you're an expectant mom, let me encourage you with this thought: Pregnancy should be worn as a badge of honor. The Lord has a special reward for you. Hang onto your hat. It's going to be a wondrous adventure.

And while you're pregnant, try to ignore those well-meaning clowns with the goofy remarks—and fight the urge to clobber those poor, clueless souls. They probably either don't know or don't remember what it's like to go weeks at a time without seeing their feet. They don't understand the frustration of uncontrollably crying over a McDonald's commercial—not to mention hardly being able to say the word "Hallmark" or even think of a "Little House on the Prairie" rerun. They can't relate to bending over to pick up a sock and wondering if their eyeballs are going to pop out. Humor them and understand that they are, yes, clueless. Spend large amounts of time in the Word of God. You'll find certain passages especially comforting. Such as, "Come … ye that LABOUR and are HEAVY LADEN, and I will give you rest" (Matthew 11:28, KJV, emphasis added).

Now a word to those of us with a few pregnancies under our belts (notice the great play on words—I'm proud of that one). When we meet up with an expectant mom, we could certainly do well to season our speech with an extra measure of love, grace, and understanding.

And shouldn't that be the goal for every one of us at all times? Our speech should always have God's love and grace sprinkled through each word. Through pregnancy, PMS, change of life—God's grace is perfectly appropriate and always available. Even in multihormonal situations, the Father can help us use loving words even in the midst of our own multihormonal situations. He can give us the grace to show grace to others. He even gives grace to love and forgive the clueless souls when we'd rather do some major clobbering instead.

Let's all remember to filter our conversation through God's Word at every stage of life. Colossians 3:12–14 says, "Therefore, as the elect of God, holy and beloved, put on tender mercies, kindness, humility, meekness, longsuffering; bearing with one another, and forgiving one another, if anyone has a complaint against another; even as Christ forgave you, so you also must do. But above all these things put on love, which is the bond of perfection" (NKJV).

Maybe we can make a point of remembering to show a little extra grace to those special hormonal women in our lives. Perhaps I should also mention here that for most of us, half the time we have an opportunity to show grace to a hormonal woman. The other half of the time we are the hormonal woman! Grace, grace, and more grace!

"And above all things have fervent love for one another, for 'love will cover a multitude of sins.' Be hospitable to one another without grumbling. As each one has received a gift, minister it to one another, as good stewards of the manifold grace of God."

1 Peter 4:8–10, NKJV

chapter twenty-eight

· · · · ·

Aren't Teens a Scream!

I made a wonderful friend when I was in the eighth grade. Her name was Judy. Our friendship survived puberty, boys, getting our driver's licenses, and even very bad perms. But I think one of the biggest tests of our friendship was when I tried to gain weight while she was trying to lose. Just in case you don't know it, when you're a teenager, the weight battle is no small matter. Foreign affairs and the national economy rank far below the weight issue when you're a teen.

I have to confess I didn't have a speck of compassion or understanding. When she asked how I stayed skinny, I would answer, "It's easy. I just don't eat." She would run from the room letting out some sort of primal scream as I sat at the table with a confused look and a Twinkie dangling out of one side of my mouth.

Twenty-something years and twenty pounds later, the primal screams are mine. If I named these twenty pounds, I think I'd have to call them "Judy's Revenge." That would make it more personal than naming the pounds after their parents, Ding Dong and Brownie. The miracle of it all is Judy and I are still great friends, despite my teenage insensitivity.

While we're on the subject of teenagers, I've made an interesting observation. Boys and girls seem to stop using vowels at around the age of thirteen. And I've noticed another amazing phenomenon. Maybe this phenomenon occurs because adults can't understand the teenage vowel-less language very well. Whatever the reason, teens seem to develop some sort of body language combined with a form of gymnastics. It's really pretty amazing. The spinning-shoulder/eye-roll combination is one of the most complicated moves in the teenager Olympics, yet I still see many master it.

All five of my children will be teenagers at the same time. Perhaps I should stop this chapter right here and we should all bow for intense, fervent prayer. … If you've finished praying, I'll continue. I know just enough about teenagers to be looking forward to these years. Okay, now you can stop laughing and go back to praying.

Thankfully, I think my children will be more compassionate and understanding than I was when I was a teenager. If not, then at least I have the comfort of knowing I have more compassion and understanding than I did back then, and maybe that will help me deal with my children tenderheartedly. I'm going to keep praying 1 Peter 3:8–9 for my family: "Finally, all of you be of one mind, having compassion for one another; love as brothers, be tenderhearted, be courteous; not returning evil for evil or reviling for reviling, but on the contrary blessing, knowing that you were called to this, that you may inherit a blessing" (NKJV).

Teens get lots of examples of selfishness, evil, and coldheartedness from the world. My goal is to let "a blessing" be the inheritance for my children. I do hope I can be a better testimony of compassion to them than I was to Judy.

You can stop by my house anytime to see if I'm meeting that goal. Don't stop if you hear primal screams.

"We should no longer be children, tossed to and fro and carried about with every wind of doctrine, by the trickery of men, in the cunning craftiness of deceitful plotting, but, speaking the truth in love, may grow up in all things into Him who is the head—Christ—from whom the whole body, joined and knit together by what every joint supplies, according to the effective working by which every part does its share, causes growth of the body for the edifying of itself in love."

Ephesians 4:14–16, NKJV

chapter twenty-nine

· · · · ·

UP Words

Words are powerful. It's amazing how placing a simple word or two in the wrong spot can convey a completely different meaning than intended. A mistaken accent here, a missed syllable there and you can find yourself in a colossal misunderstanding. As a matter of fact, even perfectly ordered words can carry sneaky double meanings that can get you into hot water.

The other day, for instance, I told my family I wanted to try out a new recipe and that I needed a guinea pig. My kids ran screaming out of the room and immediately started hiding their pets. All I wanted was someone to try my new dish! "Guinea Fricassee" was the furthest thing from my mind, believe me. I have to admit, however, I thought about smacking my lips with something like, "Mmm, tastes like chicken." Too bad the kids were already running through the house taking an animal inventory.

I'm afraid that wasn't an isolated miscommunication. These kinds of word things happen all the time around my house. Just today I told Allie to get on her homework. She sat on her book bag. Don't you just hate being misunderstood?

My nephew experienced it too. My brother, Randy, was in the car with his twelve- and thirteen-year-old boys. The talk show on the radio brought up the topic of spanking. One caller was bragging, "I got my last spanking at twelve years old when I learned I could outrun my parents." Randy had to get out at that point and put gas in the car. When he got back, his oldest son tattled, "Dad, Benny said he could outrun you!" Benny was indignant. "Did not!" The record had to be set straight. "I said anyone could outrun Dad!"

Sometimes a tough time is not necessarily a result of someone misinterpreting words. It's a result of choosing to say the wrong ones. Words seem cheap. They don't weigh anything, you can't see them, they're not fattening, and once they're off the lips there's hardly any physical evidence they've been there. But we shouldn't kid ourselves. They're potent. They can heal or hurt, build up or tear down. I've decided that words are sort of directional. The up or down of my words is my choice. Proverbs 12:25 is a directional example: "An anxious heart weighs a man down, but a kind word cheers him up."

I want to make a point of using "up" words. Words that "build up," "lift up," "cheer up"—in general "stir up" good. One of my favorite verses is Hebrews 10:24: "And let us consider one another in order to stir up love and good works" (NKJV). There are different ways to stir up. I can stir up anger, I can stir up strife, or I can stir up love and good works. Proverbs 15:1 says, "A gentle answer turns away wrath, but a harsh word stirs up anger." Not too tough to figure which is the more rewarding, is it? Proverbs 15:23 tells us that good "up" words stir up joy: "A man finds joy in giving an apt reply—and how good is a timely word!"

Words are important to the Lord. He tells us in Matthew 12:36 that people will have to give account for every careless word spoken. Every word. He also tells us in that passage that the word thing is really a heart thing. "For out of the overflow of the heart the mouth speaks" (verse 34).

Since words are important to Jesus, they need to be important to me. James 3:2 tells us that if we can control our words, our entire lives are affected. "If anyone is never at fault in what he says, he is a perfect man, able to keep his whole body in check."

Words are a giant part of my life. I write them and speak them every day. My children watch how I use them. They can also sense the direction of the words that I send their way. I want each word to go in the right direction and from the right direction—from a pure heart UP! I think I'll let Ephesians 4:29 be my word compass. "Do not let any unwholesome talk come out of your mouths, but only what is helpful for building others UP according to their needs, that it may benefit those who listen" (emphasis added).

UP words will leave a good taste in my mouth every time—not necessarily like guinea pig.

"For God did not appoint us to suffer wrath but to receive salvation through our Lord Jesus Christ. He died for us so that, whether we are awake or asleep, we may live together with him. Therefore encourage one another and build each other up, just as in fact you are doing."

1 Thessalonians 5:9–11

chapter thirty
· · · · ·
Making the Best-Dressed List

I 've had several "déjà vu" experiences lately. It's because the flower children are back! Who would've thought bell-bottoms would ever be back in style? Who would've thought that any fashion statement from the sixties would be back in style? I've always heard that if you keep everything in your closet long enough, all the fashion trends will eventually come back around. What I wasn't told was that I probably wouldn't fit it into any of them by then. I also didn't realize that I wouldn't be so interested in looking "hip" the second time around. I can't say that I'm disappointed that there are no longer any "love beads" in my jewelry box.

Still, every once in a while I have what I call a "bad closet" morning. I stand staring hypnotically into my closet waiting for a semitrendy yet sophisticated outfit to jump out at me. I stare. Nothing jumps. What to wear, what to wear?

Thankfully, my Heavenly Father has already determined what the best-dressed soul is wearing. You can't find this outfit on the shopping channel, and while operators are not standing by to take your order, I can say that the Father is always there, ready and waiting with the perfect fit for each of His children.

We're told what the best-dressed child of God is sporting in Isaiah 61:10: "I delight greatly in the Lord; my soul rejoices in my God. For he has clothed me with garments of salvation and arrayed me in a robe of righteousness." I never had to stand and stare for my garments of salvation and my robe of righteousness. As a matter of fact, they didn't even belong to me (and is there anything a gal loves more than trading clothes with a friend?). My garments of salvation and my robe of righteousness came straight from God through the

Grace to Love Without Bellyaching

righteousness of His Son, Jesus Christ. It's Jesus' robe I wear. And I must say, I look mah-velous!

We still have other wardrobe choices we can make. Colossians 3 tells us some spiritual fashion no-no's. Some of the fashion don'ts are summed up in verse 5 as "whatever belongs to your earthly nature."

Thankfully, we're not only taught the no-no's. If all we had were the "what not to wears," that could very well leave us spending the day in our spiritual underwear. Not pretty. But verse 12 tells us what to put on as God's chosen, holy, dearly loved people (those already wearing the garments of salvation and the robe of righteousness). "Clothe yourselves with compassion, kindness, humility, gentleness and patience. Bear with each other and forgive whatever grievances you may have against one another. Forgive as the Lord forgave you. And over all these virtues put on love, which binds them all together in perfect unity."

We are to be clothed in compassion, kindness, humility, gentleness, patience, forgiveness, and "over all" (not to be confused with "overalls"— that's an entirely different look) we are instructed to put on love. Love is the ultimate accessory—our single most important piece of outerwear. It pulls the entire outfit together (binds the other virtues together in "perfect unity"). Now there's a look.

Let me add that the Father doesn't leave us all dressed up with no place to go. The rest of the passage in Colossians tells us to let the Word of Christ live in us, to teach and encourage each other, singing "psalms, hymns and spiritual songs with gratitude in your hearts to God" (verse 16). We have work to do. Verse 17 tells us that whatever our work, we are to serve Jesus. "And whatever you do, whether in word or deed, do it all in the name of the Lord Jesus, giving thanks to God the Father through him. ... Whatever you do, work at it with all your heart, as working for the Lord, not for men. ... It is the Lord Christ you are serving." (verses 17, 23–24). All dressed up with great places to go!

I guess that means that I make it to God's best-dressed list when I'm putting on my work clothes. It's a great look, if I do say so myself—bell-bottoms or no bell- bottoms.

"You were taught, with regard to your former way of life, to put off your old self, which is being corrupted by its deceitful desires; to be made new in the attitude of your minds; and to put on the new self, created to be like God in true righteousness and holiness."

Ephesians 4:22–24

part seven

Grace Through His Humongous Love

*Focusing on God's
merciful love for me*

chapter thirty-one

Journey to the Bottom of My Purse

I carry the basic essentials of life in my purse. Aspirin, lipstick, hand lotion, credit cards ... you name it, it's in there. If it's not, it will be. I seem to have some sort of purse reflex. I can stuff things in there without even knowing it.

On the positive side, I found a five-dollar bill in a sneaky secret pocket last week. Even better, I found a candy bar. Now that was interesting. It was squished—almost liquefied—but it was still inside the wrapper.

Unfortunately, there are other encounters now and then that aren't exactly positive purse experiences. The other day, for example, I was making a return and I had to do an emergency receipt search at the customer-service counter. My purse stuff started spilling out. I pulled out five loose Lifesavers, an old valentine card, sunscreen, one mitten, six kid meal toys (including a minitractor with only one wheel), three keys of unknown lock origin, and a dead cricket. But no receipt. There were twelve tissues (none I would actually use), last year's Christmas list, a ticket stub to the junior-high spring concert, and the backs from four adhesive name tags.

I also found two gummy worms stuck in a hairbrush, a Denny's coupon that expired in 1997, and a plastic Easter egg. I was pretty sure the egg was older than the coupon. I shook it to see if it rattled. It did. I think I made it angry.

There was also enough purse fuzz in there to stuff a sofa pillow. How embarrassing. Inside the purse fuzz, something green and squishy caught my eye—and it frightened me. I gained courage by tossing the dead cricket and drinking the candy bar.

Grace Through His Humongous Love

Just before I dove into the fuzz, I got to the heart of my purse: my mini-Bible. It had all my family pictures tucked inside. That's when I realized everything important in life could be found in my purse.

Okay, if you want to get technical, I didn't exactly find Jesus in my handbag. But I could pull out the pictures of my husband and my children and see reminders of His gifts to me. And His Word was there. Granted, it smelled a little like Juicy Fruit, but it was a great reminder there's really no place I can go where I won't find the Lord's presence. Not one fuzz-covered place!

Psalm 139:7–10 says:

"Where can I go from your Spirit?
Where can I flee from your presence?
If I go up to the heavens, you are there;
if I make my bed in the depths, you are there.
If I rise on the wings of the dawn,
if I settle on the far side of the sea,
even there your hand will guide me,
your right hand will hold me fast."

There's no place I can go without Him—not the heavens, not the depths, not the far side of the sea. I could climb all the way inside my purse, and He would still find me there. There's nothing He doesn't know about me. The opening verses in chapter 139 remind me He knows when I'm sitting or standing, He knows my every action, word, and thought. He knows my thoughts even before I think them. He knows the contents of my purse and the contents of my heart, and He still loves me, guides me, and holds me fast.

. It's amazing to me that my Heavenly Father thinks about me—and that He thinks of me so often. Verses 17–18 say, "How precious to me are your thoughts, O God! How vast is the sum of them! Were I to count them, they would outnumber the grains of sand." He's thinking loving thoughts of you, too. If God had a wallet, not only would it be clean (nothing like my purse) but your picture would be in there, tucked in a special place reserved for those He loves.

I'm rejoicing in His love—even though I never found the receipt.

For the record, I think that green squishy thing used to be a jelly bean. I guess we'll never know. One of the kids ate it.

"Behold what manner of love the Father has bestowed on us, that we should be called children of God! Therefore the world does not know us, because it did not know Him. Beloved, now we are children of God; and it has not yet been revealed what we shall be, but we know that when He is revealed, we shall be like Him, for we shall see Him as He is. And everyone who has this hope in Him purifies himself, just as He is pure."

1 John 3:1–3, NKJV

chapter thirty-two
· · · · ·
Mercy Me

I don't have the spiritual gift of mercy. After a couple of minutes of comforting one of my children after a boo-boo, I have to fight off the strong urge to say something like, "Look, there's no bone protruding through the skin. Unless this thing needs a tourniquet, it's time to get over it and move on."

While mercy is not among my spiritual gifts, one look at my husband will tell you he's oozing with the stuff. My kids take the long way around my side of the bed when they're sick to get to his side. Then they say something like, "Dad, I think I'm going to … " No need to explain how that scenario ends, right?

In the middle of one night as we were changing the sheets on our bed, my husband cracked a smile and said, "You can tell by the mattress who has the gift of mercy in this house." He can be especially witty at 3 A.M. I answered, "Hey, I may not have the gift of mercy, but I don't think I'll be losing much sleep over it—over here on my nice, clean side of the bed."

My natural tendency is to excuse any lack of compassion I may notice in myself because "that's just not my gift." But I've also noticed God's Word gives me a different message about mercy, and even those of us who aren't specifically gifted in mercy are still called to be merciful. Yes, there is the special spiritual gift of mercy, but all of us are instructed to show mercy and compassion. Luke 6:36 is clear: "Be merciful, just as your Father is merciful."

I'm commanded to show the same kind of mercy my Heavenly Father shows. Wow, take a look at His mercy! It's the very reason I have new life. "In his great mercy he has given us new birth into a living hope through the resurrection of Jesus Christ from the dead" (1 Peter 1:3).

I'm instructed to be merciful as the Father is merciful, and the Father,

Grace Through His Humongous Love

according to Micah 7:18, delights to show mercy. He doesn't merely show mercy, He loves showing mercy. If that's not clear enough, Micah 6:8 spells out my life instructions: "And what does the Lord require of you? To act justly and to love mercy and to walk humbly with your God." Not just show mercy, love mercy.

What about the consequences of refusing to be merciful? The Scripture isn't quiet about that one either: "Judgment without mercy will be shown to anyone who has not been merciful. Mercy triumphs over judgment!" (James 2:13). Who needs extra judgment? Not me. Mercy is the winner over judgment every time.

One of the triumphs of mercy is blessing. Did you notice mercy made it to the Top-Nine list of "blesseds" in Matthew 5? There is great blessing in showing mercy. Verse 7 says, "Blessed are the merciful, for they will be shown mercy." Okay, these particular blessings may not necessarily include a barf-free mattress. But they're grand blessings, nonetheless.

If I try motherhood with a completely empty mercy bank, at the very least it can result in some pretty meager loving, Kodak moments. But God is rich in mercy. I can go to His throne and boldly ask, then make a mercy withdrawal from His account. The amazing thing is even after my withdrawal, He has no less mercy. He stays forever mercy-wealthy! And mercy, grace, and love are a bit of a package deal, so I can walk away with the whole parcel. It happens as I fully trust in His ability to make me the merciful person He wants me to be.

Our Heavenly Father is the supplier of mercy, grace, and love, and He is the example. Ephesians 2:4–5 says that "because of his great love for us, God, who is rich in mercy, made us alive with Christ even when we were dead in transgressions—it is by grace you have been saved."

The Lord Almighty Himself says to "show mercy and compassion to one another" in Zechariah 7:9. So that's my mercy goal. James 3:17 also tells me it's wise to be merciful. As a matter of fact, it says wisdom is "full of mercy." That's also part of my goal. Not half-mercy. Full. Even in a situation where a tourniquet is completely unnecessary.

"For He who is mighty has done great things for me,
And holy is His name.
And His mercy is on those who fear Him
From generation to generation."

Luke 1:49–50, NKJV

chapter thirty-three
. . . . .

What's for Dinner?

There I was again … staring blankly into the pantry, thumping my fingers on the door. What would I scrounge together for dinner this time? It's not that there wasn't any food in there. As a matter of fact, every shelf was packed. But how could I make a meal for a family of seven from half a bag of noodles, the creams from a box of assorted chocolates (all pinched), and a packet of sauce mix from a missing box of Rice-A-Roni? I dug up some cocoa mix, a box of potato buds and a handful of chocolate chips. I thought I'd hit the jackpot when I found a dozen hot sauce packets from Taco Bell, some stale crackers and a box of Kit 'N Kaboodle—no wait, that last one was cat food.

I couldn't even see a microwavable casserole coming together, so I ate the handful of chocolate chips for strength and moved from the pantry to the fridge. There were about the same number of possibilities in there. Dozens of containers but none I was willing to actually open. Through the clearish one I could make out some fuzzy purple ravioli. I didn't remember ever having ravioli. (Okay, that was scary.) Wasn't there anything in there I could microwave for dinner?

You might have guessed I support heavy use of the microwave oven. I realized I might have taken it too far the other day when we were getting ready for company and I actually had to dust the stove. I thought about getting rid of my stove altogether, but a friend told me I was deranged. ("De-ranged." Get it?) Besides, it's a great place to hide dirty dishes if company stops by unexpectedly.

The "What's for dinner?" question remains a toughie for me. Even when my pantry is filled with wonderfully zap-able cardboard boxes, I find it difficult to choose. I'm so glad my Heavenly Father didn't have to stare into the "pantry" of the world, trying to put together something redeemable. No, I picture Jesus Himself saying, "I'll take that one," as He plucked me out to make me into something special.

I'm not special because of anything I can do, mind you. I'm special because the Lord chose me and because He lives in me. Ephesians 1:4 says, "just as He chose us in Him before the foundation of the world, that we should be holy and without blame before Him in love" (NKJV). Verse 10 says that "He might gather together in one all things in Christ" (NKJV). Gathering together. Almost sounds like a casserole, doesn't it? I'm so thankful our all-powerful Father looked into His grand pantry and started His holy gathering "in Christ."

If you are "in Christ," you can picture your Father plucking you out, too. Isn't it great to be chosen by the One who matters most? You are His special creation and He treasures you.

And spoil like that ravioli? No way. The holiness and blamelessness verse 4 says is ours comes straight from him, "in love." All the blame for our sin is traded for holiness. No blame. No spoiling. No fooling!

And if we've trusted in Christ, He has sealed us by His Holy Spirit. We're wrapped and sealed in him with a seal that's tighter than any plastic wrap, better than a Ziploc and more dependable than any burped container. "In Him you also trusted, after you heard the word of truth, the gospel of your salvation; in whom also, having believed, you were sealed with the Holy Spirit of promise" (verse 13, NKJV).

There's no safer place to have your soul than safely sealed by the Holy Spirit of promise. It's not a "hope so" seal. It's not a "maybe" seal. As sure as yellow and blue make green, you can count on the sure-seal of His promise.

There's a wonderful, airtight comfort to our souls there in the fridge if we don't overlook it. And I love it when I can find a lesson in my pantry—even when I can't find a dinner in there. My lesson that day also became a sweet reminder of how very blessed I am. That blessing called for celebration. I decided to celebrate by calling 1-800-PIZZAGUY.

Still, you're welcome to drop by for dinner sometime. I promise not to serve "Kaboodle Casserole." By the way, if you should stop by unexpectedly, please don't look in the oven.

"just as He chose us in Him before the foundation of the world, that we should be holy and without blame before Him in love, having predestined us to adoption as sons by Jesus Christ to Himself, according to the good pleasure of His will, to the praise and the glory of His grace, by which He made us accepted in the Beloved."

Ephesians 1:4–6, NKJV

chapter thirty-four

· · · · ·

Everything Has a Home

Y ou wouldn't believe the destruction five kids and two cats can generate in a family room. It amazes me that there are only seven people in the family, yet I can find three dozen shoes in there at any given time. It's like that little cobbler elf is manufacturing tennies under my sofa. My children keep blaming the cats.

There's a reason that I never invite the governor over for dinner. Okay, there are several reasons. One is that the governor doesn't know me. But the chief reason is that I'm afraid one look at the family room would result in the entire house being declared a disaster area. I have to wonder, though, if that would get me some sort of federal funding to help with the cleanup. Hmmm.

I've been trying for around a dozen years to teach my kids that every item in the house—even a shoe—has its own "home," and that we would all do well to put each item away in its home. Shoes are supposed to have a home in the closet.

I'm sad to say that my "everything has a home" program hasn't been all that successful in the family room. To be honest, it hasn't been any too effective in the other rooms either. Last week, for instance, I got a surprise in my bathroom. I was getting ready for one of those relaxing Calgon-type moments. At my house, my giant tub is not necessarily a hygiene thing. It's more like therapy. I was easing into the tub for some therapy when I got a surprise. I sat on a triceratops. A purple one. Did I mention my surprise? I think I nearly had a coronary episode.

You might find this hard to believe, but I've decided not to sweat the triceratops in the tub. I'm not even letting the shoefactory/familyroom bug me on an ongoing basis. I'm working toward saving my "episodes" for bigger issues.

Grace Through His Humongous Love

In the light of eternity, what's one purple triceratops? My home here is temporary. I do have a real home. My real home is triceratops-free. Even better, it's a home without sin of any kind. I love that. Second Peter 3:13 calls it a home of righteousness. "But in keeping with his promise we are looking forward to a new heaven and a new earth, the home of righteousness."

When we keep our eyes on our permanent home instead of this shoe-filled, dinosaur-laden one, we gain a much better perspective and a much better attitude about every tub obstacle. We might even find ourselves grinning in the midst of a purple triceratops situation. Well, at least after a triceratops situation.

Romans 8:18 tells us that these plastic dinosaur situations can't compare with what's in store for us in our new home. "I consider that our present sufferings are not worth comparing with the glory that will be revealed in us." And verse 22 says, "We know that the whole creation has been groaning as in the pains of childbirth right up to the present time." Groaning? That I understand. The next verse mentions how we, too, "groan inwardly as we wait eagerly,"—waiting for the redemption of our bodies. (A little FYI: Sitting on a triceratops might cause some outward groaning, too.)

Verses 24–25 say, "For in this hope we were saved. But hope that is seen is no hope at all. Who hopes for what he already has? But if we hope for what we do not yet have, we wait for it patiently."

I want to be found waiting patiently for that glorious new home that I haven't yet seen. I want to be found waiting patiently through any and all dinosaur and miscellaneous shoe situations.

So it's a new week here in my temporary home. It's a week filled with the wonderful hope in a future home of righteousness. This week, although I still haven't completely given up on the "everything has a home" cleaning method, I've decided to focus on the goal of being found waiting more patiently. I'm just glad that I made that decision before yesterday's Calgon trip. This time I stepped on a tank.

"For you did not receive a spirit that makes you a slave again to fear, but you received the Spirit of sonship. And by him we cry, "Abba, Father." The Spirit himself testifies with our spirit that we are God's children. Now if we are children, then we are heirs—heirs of God and co-heirs with Christ, if indeed we share in his sufferings in order that we may also share in his glory.

"I consider that our present sufferings are not worth comparing with the glory that will be revealed in us. ... We know that the whole creation has been groaning as in the pains of childbirth right up to the present time. Not only so, but we ourselves, who have the firstfruits of the Spirit, groan inwardly as we wait eagerly for our adoption as sons, the redemption of our bodies. For in this hope we were saved. But hope that is seen is no hope at all. Who hopes for what he already has? But if we hope for what we do not yet have, we wait for it patiently."

Romans 8:15–18, 22–25

chapter thirty-five

· · · · ·

Storing Up

T he grocery store is an adventure. Would it frighten you to know that my five kids consume almost two gallons of milk and a loaf and a half of bread every day? I'm pretty pleased with myself when I can refrain from making pitiful moaning noises as the checker hits total and hands me a six-foot receipt. It's always good for me to include smelling salts in the week's booty.

The checkers are a little clueless. They seldom realize I'm purchasing food for only a week. Most of them assume I'm stockpiling for some impending disaster. They're not totally off base. The impending disaster comes as I try to fit an aisle's worth of groceries into a tenth-of-an-aisle-sized kitchen.

My ten-year-old daughter helped me with the putting-away process last time. "Mom, I can't make the new groceries fit into the refrigerator with all this other stuff in here."

She was right. "Okay, Allie, how about taking out the stuff we can't eat so we can make some room?"

She gave me a look of fear and doom. "You want me to clean out the refrigerator?"

Allie pulled out one of the plastic containers like she was handling a vial of toxic waste. She wouldn't take her eyes off it—her eyebrows were somewhere around her hairline. "Mom, there's something in here." She looked frightened, then she looked disgusted, and then … sort of amazed. "I have no idea what this is."

"Just some leftovers," I tried to reassure her. Then I peered into the container and studied it myself. That's when I realized I had no idea what it was either. Do you know how unnerving it can be to find leftovers growing in the fridge yet have no clue what they're left over from? "Could this have been chicken?" Allie asked. "I think I see a beak."

We stared for a while, but eventually just shuddered and tossed it. We also tossed a brown, slimy bag that must have been lettuce in another life, some spaghetti that seemed to have made its own meatballs, and a little surprise butter dish that contained something that was definitely not butter. Before long the old junk was out and the fridge was filled with fresh new groceries. I don't think Allie was too traumatized by the ordeal—although come to think of it, she has asked for fast food a lot lately.

The entire episode made me think about how much we can miss spiritually. We sometimes miss the new because we've neglected to clean out the old. The Lord wants to supply the new, but we tend to hang on to the fleshly old stuff. Jealousy, for instance, can be as putrid as month-old chicken. Left as it is, it will mold and ferment just like that container of "whatever" that Allie and I threw away. Then it squeezes out the peace that's ready and waiting "in the grocery bag." Isn't it sad to imagine the Father saying, "Oops, no place for this peace in here—too full of rottenness." Proverbs 14:30 says, "A heart at peace gives life to the body, but envy rots the bones." Are you picturing a petrified chicken bone with me?

Jealousy and envy start cultivating when we stop celebrating the successes of others. It's a rejoicing opportunity left to mold into selfishness. The jealousy story boils down to the unspoken selfish question: "Why can't I have that blessing instead?"

Make room for peace. Make room for Jesus. Let Him fill every corner. He brings with His peace the whole list of fruit from Galatians 5:22, including love, joy, goodness, and more. This fruit doesn't need preservatives—it never shrivels, never rots, never even needs a seal-and-burp container—and it's healthy! It's life to the body! Now those are the kinds of provisions we really want to store up.

Galatians 5:19–21 lists the rotten things His fruit can replace. Paul named them as "the acts of the sinful nature"—and guess what moldy weaknesses made the list? You can find jealousy is in verse 20 and envy made the list in 21.

Here's some good news to store up. As we make room for Jesus and stockpile His virtues, we begin to automatically chuck jealousy, envy, and the like. It's a wonderful surprise to find that even after stuffing His long and wonderful list of virtues into our lives, believe it or not, there's still plenty of room for more goodness left over!

Sorry, did I say, "leftover"? Don't worry. That has nothing to do with moldy chicken.

"But if you harbor bitter envy and selfish ambition in your hearts, do not boast about it or deny the truth. Such 'wisdom' does not come down from heaven but is earthly, unspiritual, of the devil. For where you have envy and selfish ambition, there you find disorder and every evil practice. But the wisdom that comes from heaven is first of all pure; then peace-loving, considerate, submissive, full of mercy and good fruit, impartial and sincere. Peacemakers who sow in peace raise a harvest of righteousness."

James 3:14–18

A Personal Note From the Author

Heart: My friends, I truly do know what it's like to find that your preschooler has thrown up sock fuzz and red Koolaid in the toybox—sometime around last Thursday. My heart's desire in sharing *Amusing Grace* with you is to remind you that you're not in this alone. It's also my desire that this book helps enable you to take the life-giving medicine of God's Word with a spoonful of heart-lifting laughter—and maybe even put a bit of an eternal spin on the everyday calamity as you find the grace to shrug away some of those toxic toybox traumas. Yes, there's grace even in the toybox!

Soul: Colossians 2:2-3 sums up the purpose in writing *Amusing Grace*:

"My purpose is that they may be encouraged in heart and united in love, so that they may have the full riches of complete understanding, in order that they may know the mystery of God, namely, Christ, in whom are hidden all the treasures of wisdom and knowledge." (NIV)

My hope is that this book points to Christ in every little happening and in every huge happening. Before we even think of the question, Jesus is the answer.

Mind: Need more? Wonderful! If we want to set our minds on things above and not get hung up on earthly things (Colossians 3:2), we need to feed our minds the right kind of diet. If I were to write, "The Care and Feeding of a Healthy Mind," I think I would have to include these tasty morsels:

Slices of Life by Ellie Lofaro
Simply the Savior by Nancy Parker Brummel
Lord Change Me! by Evelyn Christenson
Princess to Princess by Kathy Collard Miller

Strength: It's my hope that this book is a blessing to you, just as you have blessed me by choosing it. *Amusing Grace* is designed for a cover-to-cover read when you have one of those sleepless nights, or for a snippet here and a snippet there—whenever a grace-need hits. The chapters can even be used as a day's devotion on those busy, fast-food days. Each one contains scripture and an extra passage at the end for further study. Enjoy, and may you continue to grow in his grace!

Father, I pray that you will use *Amusing Grace* to encourage the reader's heart. Remind her of the honor of her calling, even in the middle of wiping little noses or taxiing teens. I pray that she will fully know how completely precious she is to you. When she's tired, Lord, please hold her up with your strength. When she's grouchy, lend her your gentleness. When she's down, please give her the sweet gift of a good giggle and the comfort that comes from resting in you.

I pray also that you will remind her of the treasure of your loving grace. Thank you for the amazing way you allow us to be united in your love—brought together in heart—because we have your indwelling presence in common. May the reader "have the full riches of complete understanding," and may she enjoy the precious knowledge of the mystery of your grace given to us in your Son, Jesus Christ.

Thank you for the work of grace you're continuing in our lives. And thanks for making so much of it such great and adventurous fun.

In the Name of Jesus,

Rhonda Rhea

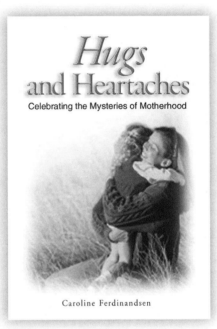